BRAVE NEW YOU

12 Dynamic Strategies for Saying
What You Want & Being Who You Are

Mary Valentis, Ph.D. & John Valentis, Ph.D.

NEW HARBINGER PUBLICATIONS, INC.

Publisher's Note

This publication is designed to provide accurate and authoritative information in regard to the subject matter covered. It is sold with the understanding that the publisher is not engaged in rendering psychological, financial, legal, or other professional services. If expert assistance or counseling is needed, the services of a competent professional should be sought.

Distributed in the U.S.A. by Publishers Group West; in Canada by Raincoast Books; in Great Britain by Airlift Book Company, Ltd.; in South Africa by Real Books, Ltd.; in Australia by Boobook; and in New Zealand by Tandem Press.

Copyright © 2001 by Mary Valentis and John Valentis
New Harbinger Publications, Inc.
5674 Shattuck Avenue
Oakland, CA 94609

Cover design by Salmon Studios
Cover image: Richard Seagraves/Photonica
Edited by Jueli Gastwirth
Text design by Tracy Marie Powell-Carlson

Library of Congress Catalog Card Number: 01-132294

ISBN 1-57224-259-0 Paperback

Printed in the United States of America

New Harbinger Publications' Web site address: www.newharbinger.com

03   02   01
10   9   8   7   6   5   4   3   2   1
First printing

To my mother, Elizabeth, and to my sister, Barbara.

  —Mary

To the memories of my father, Denis, and my friend, Arnold.

  —John

Contents

Acknowledgments

Writing this book was a daring adventure. We had collaborated before on workshops, a radio show, and media appearances, but working together on a book required another level of bravery and the resolve to find new ways of communicating and playing to each other's strengths and individual expertise. Our family and friends, many of whom are acknowledged below, inspired and moved us, sharing their stories and providing examples of how to live bravely. We are extremely grateful to our editor, Jueli Gastwirth, a woman who exemplifies the values of being who you are and saying what you want, in addition to being a consummate professional and talented collaborator.

John acknowledges his life partner and soul mate, Mary; his mentors, Dr. David Viscott, Dr. Joy Browne, Ruth Franklin, Lloyd Glauberman, Ph.D., and Jim McGettigan, Ph.D.; and the following friends, family, and colleagues: John Gillespie, Charles Anderson, Charles Stephens, Bob Sager, Christine Gilbert, Zina, Sylvia Thaler, Charles Slap, his uncles, Jack and Jerry, and especially his patients of twenty-five years who have taught him so much about bravery and the human condition.

Mary acknowledges John, whose deep love and courage encourage her to risk and change every day; and the following friends and colleagues who, in their own ways, have served as inspirational muses, role models and mentors, dear friends and companions: Lisa White and Ian Pinkerton, Shirley Belden, Mary Martin, Dan Smirlock, Barbara L. Cohen, Shirley Gordon, Marcia Scharfman, Rena Button, Diane Goodman, Louise Marwill, Barbara McNamee, Nancy Liddle, Delia Pitkin, Ellie and Marvin Posner, M.D., Mary and Albert Yunich, M.D., Bea and Bob Herman, Laurie Jacobson, Penelope Benson-Wright, Marta Greene, Rex Ruthman, Carline Davenport, Arvilla Cline, Rev. Sandra Hulsie, Anne and Mark Wang, M.D., Matt and Phoebe Bender, Xenia Stephens, Carol Southern, Joan Curry, Elizabeth Nathan, Kathlyn Hatch, Chris D'Elia, Dana and Bill Kennedy, Don Faulkner, and most especially her dear friends Joanna, Charles Anderson, Ira Mendleson, Carey Christie, Phillip, and Tom.

Introduction

Traveling toward the Brave New You

Life shrinks and expands in proportion to one's courage.

—Anaïs Nin

There is nothing more appealing, and at the same time, more threatening than a brave woman, for she is self-possessed in mind and spirit. Women look to her for inspiration. Men who are secure with their own identity find her captivating. A brave woman earns respect and notoriety, not because she's a superstar, but because she knows who she is, what she believes in, and how to effectively communicate both.

The brave woman's composure emanates from a core of strength and integrity. Her values, beliefs, and actions are in harmony. She is creative, idiosyncratic, and strong-willed. She primarily is more concerned with honesty and free expression than with appearances and others' expectations. Her no-nonsense manner coupled with her innate natural appeal upset the status quo and traditional notions of womanhood, femininity, power, and submission. She tests life's limits and recognizes her gifts and abilities. The world doesn't define a brave women; she defines herself and her place in the world.

Bravery is the spark that can ignite the fires of passion and purpose in every woman. Bravery will bestow you with presence and authenticity without pretense. It will open up possibilities that once seemed unthinkable to you, propel you toward your destiny, and send you down paths you wouldn't before have dared to explore. The truth is that no matter what your life is like, you already are a brave woman. She's there inside you—poised and waiting to emerge.

One night actor-director Jodie Foster was interviewed on *Larry King Live* (Dec. 4, 1999) about her movie *Anna and the King*. At one point, King asked her: "Why do you refuse to disclose the name of your baby's father?" Foster replied, "I came here to talk about my film, Larry, not my private life." Foster had been gracious and forthcoming in her responses up to that point. When King touched on a personal area that she considers off limits, however, she backed him off politely and steered him back to the film she was promoting.

In the show's final segment, the actor Robert J. Downey, Jr., came up. "What do you think about your good friend?" King ventured, referring to the talented young actor who was serving time in a Los Angeles County jail for cocaine possession. Foster considered the question, looked up at King and said in clear, well-considered language: "He deserves to be where he is. He's learning there are consequences to his actions." This time, Foster was willing to talk on the record even if it meant censuring her friend's self-destructive behavior on air.

Of course, as with any celebrity/fan relationship, it is impossible to know the "real Jodie Foster." Yet the actress' public persona that night closely resembled many of the brave woman characters she portrays and directs on film. Foster's businesslike precision, the intensity and self-possession she projects, the willingness to assert her boundaries, the appeal, wit, intelligence, and openness of these characters most likely carry over into her real life or vice versa. Larry King had conducted the interview, but there was no mistaking that Jodie Foster had been in charge.

Bravery and You

You might be asking yourself, what does Jodie Foster have to do with me? She's the product of a Yale education, a Renaissance woman, an Oscar winner, a single mother who can afford full-time help. You may be telling yourself that being brave is for those "other women," women who seem brighter, more talented, and luckier than you are, or women who have come from families who have made it easy for them to succeed and be brave. You might also think that being brave is reserved for celebrities and professional women who have it all together.

Bravery is a *necessity*—not a luxury—for women who are shooting for the top. Jodie Foster is successful because she was brave enough to go after what she wanted and obviously has worked on maintaining her ideas and values, despite all her notoriety and commercial success. Women like Foster, highly trained Olympic athletes, judges, senators, astronauts, and others have gotten where they are precisely because they were asserting their bravery.

They risked failure, they exposed their ambition and desire, and they broke through gender stereotypes and persisted while realizing their dreams and goals in a culture that rewards men more than women. Texas Senator Kay Bailey Hutchinson (2001) puts it this way: "My advice for women who aspire to high office is that they need to learn how to lose, and be brave enough to fail. Men learn to lose in sports, but [women] don't learn how to fall down and get up, and fall down and get up, and do it again until one game you score and win."

You can't buy bravery; no one can give it to you. Bravery doesn't come from wealth or privilege, luck, or having great parents (although your parents can help put you on the right track to become a brave woman). Bravery comes from developing confidence in your powers and from doing the right thing for you and for others. It protects you and enables you to stand up for that which you believe. A brave woman knows that not taking a risk is the greatest risk of all. You may not know it yet, but you too are capable of radiating *self-possessed bravery*.

Women's Bravery: The Way It Was

Traveling by plane from the East to the West Coast, you fly over the Great Divide, with awe-inspiring views of the Rockies' snowy caps, the deserts, and the ravines. Imagine what kind of courage it took for pioneer women and men to cross the country in a Conestoga wagon. It took fortitude, physical courage, extraordinary bravery, and a willingness to always look beyond, toward the next mountain, the next horizon. Those pioneers battled harsh weather extremes, animal and human foes, sickness, death, and more. They surmounted unimaginable obstacles and, urged on by their hearts and minds to survive the passage west, reached the golden state of California.

In American history, there are vivid legends and lore about women's bravery. These often are stories of survival and sacrifice, memoirs, and diary entries that paint pictures of brave women: the midwife sloshing through the snow in winter carrying her medicinal bag of herbs from house to house and delivering babies under primitive conditions; the loneliness of the captain's wife pacing atop her widows' walks in Old New England, scanning the seas for her mate's ship; the defiant bravery of a princess who threw herself across the body of her lover, an action that saved him from certain death at the hands of the princess' father.

Struggling to overcome oppression has defined bravery in women's history. Pioneers like Elizabeth Cady Stanton, Lucretia Mott, and Susan B. Anthony battled and won the right to vote. In the 1970s, their feminist granddaughters had the courage to identify and expose in feminism's second wave what Betty Friedan (1984) called "the dirty little secret that had no name": the fact that all women are not fulfilled being mothers and homemakers. Later Gloria Steinem courageously characterized the "ghetto" of women's work outside the home and championed legislation that would ensure equal pay for equal work, a struggle that continues today.

Struggle, sacrifice, and fighting back is one class of bravery: it includes endurance, the will to survive, mental and physical grit, the kind of gutting it out required to survive a climb in the high peaks or to run a marathon.

Women's bravery also has meant being a "first": the first woman to swim the English channel, the first woman to fly solo across the Atlantic Ocean, the first woman to pilot the *Challenger* spaceship, or the first woman to become U.S. attorney general. Bravery indeed, but these brave instances are experienced only by a select few.

Lastly, bravery for women is not necessarily ego-driven bravado, gutsy and/or "ballsy," as is often portrayed in prevailing male-oriented media models for bravery. That's not to say, however, that women's bravery is quiet or suffering in silence.

At the Core of Bravery: The Babushka

At an outdoor mall in New York, there was a boutique that sold nothing but babushka dolls. The shop's shelves and glass cases were filled with at least seventy-five versions of these brightly painted wooden dolls that can be taken apart to reveal small dolls fitting inside one another. You may have one yourself. The babushka, or matryoshka doll, is a symbol of Russian folk art known all over the world. The dolls are usually displayed in a series, lined up in an ascending row from the largest to the smallest. They are all hollow on the inside, except for the last doll that remains a solid little piece of wood bearing the same image and decoration as the others, except she can't break apart.

The babushka doll is the best embodiment of the process for becoming brave, a technique that involves discarding and exfoliating the outer layers and protective shells to arrive at a woman's true, brave self.

What Is Bravery?

- Contrary to popular belief, bravery is achieved by becoming "naked" rather than shielded with protective armor.

- To be brave is to risk becoming vulnerable, stripped of false beliefs about yourself and the world, exposed to what you really believe in, and in touch with what you want to pursue.

- Embracing and exercising your bravery has nothing to do with outer trappings, putting on armor, a college degree, a professional résumé, or being glamorous.

- Becoming brave is closing the gap between what you think and believe in and what you say and do.

- Traversing the frontiers of your inner landscape, shedding myths and misconceptions about yourself and what it means to be a woman at the horizon of the twenty-first century is brave.

- Bravery is a willingness to eliminate the limitations of gender stereotypes that narrow any woman's possibilities.

- Becoming brave is eradicating dependent, disempowering, self-sacrificing behaviors and replacing them with self-assertions—speaking up for yourself and following your personal dreams in a dynamic and modulated way.

As you begin to let go of inappropriate guilt and guilt-inducing thoughts, you will sanction your novel ideas and actions and smash through old patterns and fears that have prevented you from being a genuinely brave woman. Your newfound bravery will stop you from being disingenuous, embolden you to think and act with natural candor, and allow you to stay cool under pressure or criticism.

A Blueprint to Bravery

Brave New You is your blueprint to bravery, a step-by-step plan that takes you on an encounter with your brave, essential self. As you progress through the book's twelve strategies, every brave step brings you toward the realization of your personal goals and true life's mission.

The Process toward Bravery

Your process for becoming brave begins by revealing the most accessible and available part of yourself. In chapter 1 and 2, you will open your outer "doll," working with your biography and family history, to discover where you've been, where you are, and where you're going. In chapter 3, you will cut through the myths and misconceptions that hold you back. You will uncover in chapter 4 the secrets you hide, even from yourself. Open the next doll in chapter 5 and you will deal with your deepest fears. In chapter 6, you'll discover your personality type, and what drives your thinking and behavior.

In chapter 7, you will write a mission statement and set your personal priorities, and in chapter 8, you will unpack your anger "baggage." In chapter 9, you'll discover the techniques of the bold risk-taker who acts despite any fears and doubts. Come upon the brave little doll snuggled in the heart of all the other ones, and you will arrive at the center of your being. Your bravery originates from this core. In the final chapters of the book, you encounter your inner landscape and the self that lives there (chapter 10), you will learn to trust your own intuition, thoughts, and judgment (chapter 11), and to rely on the power of the brave new you (chapter 12).

Along the way, you may notice other brave women inspiring you: young women who fight for what they want and what they believe in; women just starting over in their seventies; women who want to create congruency between the woman they present to the world and the woman they truly are inside.

Knowing You Are Brave

By the time you finish this book, you will

- Be able to say no or refuse someone's request without feeling guilty, and say yes because it's your choice;

- Believe you have the right to change your mind or direction with whatever you do;

- Accept your emotions as a barometer of where you stand and how you feel;

- Be true to your convictions and beliefs;

- Express your intelligence and creativity;

- Make an honest appraisal of your circumstances;

- Find your true mission in life; and

- Be inspired to fulfill your dreams and ambitions.

The power and force of your bravery are determined by how honest, truthful, and genuine you are with yourself, with the world, and with others. In a sense, everyone is a babushka doll, presenting his or her outer shells to the world. People hide their authentic selves and censor their words and emotions because they are caught up, afraid to appear too bold, too aggressive, too shy, too greedy, too mean, too sarcastic, too "over the top" in any way. After reading *Brave New You*, however, you'll be reminded that being who you are and saying what you want is true women's liberation.

More than Two Choices

Most of you are somewhat familiar with Robert Frost's (1964) poem, "The Road Not Taken." In that poem, Frost describes the choices all of us have as travelers through life. You remember the first line: "Two roads diverged in a yellow wood."

The first road, Frost suggests, is the option to conform and take the path most people follow, the dusty, well-trodden road of conformity, compliance, and settling for less. The second road or choice in life is to strike out on one's own and venture down the road less traveled, which is the choice of the poem's speaker.

But isn't there a third choice? There is, according to a young woman from California who wrote about this particular Frost poem in a high school class. As she handed in her paper, she asked her teacher: "Why do we have to choose? You come to a fork in the road, there seem to be two choices, but can't I just keep going straight?"

Becoming brave is being able to ask that question; seeing that there are more than one, two, or three choices, and then deciding whether to go down one path, the other one, or straight into the woods. The pages that follow provide a framework for choosing and deciding to fully be yourself in all circumstances. They are an invitation to the brave new you.

Chapter 1

Go Back to Grab Your Future Now

Where You've Been, Where You Are, Where You're Going

As far back as she could remember, she had always wanted to be a heroine.

—Jane Mendelsohn

Dynamic strategy No. 1 is to rediscover the emotional bravery and self-assertion of your girlhood. Your archive of childhood memories, when many of you said what you wanted and acted in spontaneous and brave ways, will connect you with your essential self. Your history and memories are the cornerstone for realizing the brave new you.

It has been well documented that very few girls get past adolescence with their innate sense of bravery intact. There can be many reasons for this reverse: fear of failure and/or success, the desire to please, the drive to seem feminine and adapt to the norms of the dominant male culture, the refusal to compete with men, a preteen loss of esteem, and more.

Mary Pipher (1994), author of *Reviving Ophelia*, makes the point that even when adolescent girls do resist the pressure to look or act in a certain way, the issues are so complicated that "strength is labeled weakness and vice versa." According to Pipher, early adolescence is a time when "many of the battles for the self are won or lost" (264).

Brave women are either made or break at this crucial age and growth period, between the ages of nine and fourteen. Some women have always dreamed big dreams, and, since childhood, have directed their energies and focused their passions on a life's mission. Barbara Kerr (1997) documents the childhoods and characteristics of these rugged individualists in her study *Smart Girls: A New Psychology of Girls, Women and Giftedness.* Women like Eleanor Roosevelt, Margaret Mead, Katherine Hepburn, Georgia O'Keefe, Maya Angelou, and others all eschewed gender limitations, fell in love with ideas, and later found romance through their work.

Circumstances forced some of Kerr's "eminent women" to spend time alone, or go to same-sex schools, or to be unpopular, awkward, unattractive, independent (81–90). Interestingly, these particular women turned these "deficits" into assets, and escaped the trap that the majority of gifted women fall into: holding back.

Looks-consciousness and sex-consciousness seduce many young women to conform. When they conform and buy into beauty and sex myths, they start to doubt their opinions, question their attractiveness and "likeability," check their outspokenness at the classroom door, inhibit their voices, and generally drive their intelligence and spunk underground.

Because of this loss, many women discard their dreams, tone down their spirits, and relegate their lives to the wishes of others with few of their own needs being met. While they don't literally drown themselves in a bed of flowers like Ophelia in Shakespeare's play, *Hamlet*, many young women give up on themselves and their future before it begins, prostrating their dreams on the altar of self-sacrifice, so that others may achieve what they deny for themselves.

The brave woman's ultimate project is to recover and blend the curious, risk-taking, genderless, independent, comfortable-in-her-skin girl crusader that she was at nine or ten with her adult woman's indomitable will and self-possession.

Girlhood Bravery

There was a time when you were brave. You rode bareback on a pony or painted bright blue and yellow blobs on a wall. You double dared your friend to jump from a high dune and raced the guys down the mountain on skis. Before she was three, Mary's little sister would toddle naked (without self-consciousness) into her parents' formal dinner party to the delight of all the guests. And once we found her in the garden eating a worm that fascinated her.

Helen: A Brave New Path

Some girls have always been brave. As a little girl, Helen was "fat and tomboyish," a self-portrait that's hard to square with the way she looks today: a svelte, high-cheekboned woman wearing a stylish leather jacket and tight jeans. Helen's father didn't value women; he thought women "had it pretty good" staying home and taking care of the house and children.

At age twelve, when her parents decided to sign her up for a nonacademic track in high school, Helen rebelled. "My family wanted me to be a secretary. Not that there's anything wrong with being a secretary, but I didn't want to limit my choices. We were the 'poor relatives' in the family. I had seen how money and education could enrich life and, frankly, my mother had a life I didn't want." Helen started World War III in the house over the issue of her schooling. "I was very aggressive and stubborn," she claims. After many arguments and battles, Helen got her way and filled out the application. In high school she was on her own. "I had no guidance from home, I couldn't find a mentor, so I bumbled along." Helen's bumbling took her through a combined college/nursing school where she majored in psychiatric nursing.

Today, Helen's childhood inspires and influences her. Happily married to an attorney, the adult Helen is pleasing herself more and wisely choosing her battles. To rekindle her bravery, she relies on the memory of when she was twelve years old and fought her father for the right to choose her education path. And she consistently works to find her *emotional middle ground.*

The Emotional Middle Ground

Finding the emotional middle ground is being assertive rather than unduly passive or aggressive. This can be particularly difficult for women who, during adolescence, have buried the emotional bravery and self-assertions of their girlhoods. When these same women re-engage with their lost selves—which they inevitably will do as adults—the difficult childhood feelings they've suppressed re-emerge with a vengeance.

These pent-up emotions are unsettling and hard to face. Some women simply push down their emotions. When they do this, these uncomfortable and unacceptable emotions show themselves as "uncontrollable" behaviors and compulsions—eating disorders, drug and alcohol abuse, needless spending, and other forms of reckless risk-taking. It takes a great deal of courage to confront what you really feel, because it may upset your "good girl" image. Many women hold on to that image, its false illusions, and hollow center all their lives. "Being a good girl" is a cover for not dealing with feelings and behaviors that unite the human race.

Mapping Your Girlhood

Your earliest memories—the thoughts you associate with your girlhood—are the starting point to recover your bravery. Do the work in this section on your computer or on a specially designated pad of paper or journal.

First, create a time line beginning with the date of your birth and ending with the date you consider the cutoff time for your girlhood. This date will probably fall between your eleventh and thirteenth year depending on how mature you were emotionally and physically. As you answer the following questions, write specific topics and/or themes on the time line nearest to the numbers of the age(s) when you experienced them. If you encountered recurring emotions, thoughts, or images in girlhood, list the items near each age during which you remember experiencing them.

1. What images and thoughts come to mind from this time period?

2. Which incidents bring out your happiest thoughts?

3. Which incidents saddened and frustrated you?

4. Do you think you were loved and supported?

5. Did you feel neglected, unsupported, unloved?

6. What frightened you?

7. What experiences brought out your confidence and bravery?

8. Overall, how would you describe the thoughts and feelings you have about your girlhood?

9. How do you think your girlhood affected your beliefs, attitudes, and actions to this day?

10. What made you brave? What caused you to lose your nerve and courage?

11. How did it feel to be brave?

12. How did you feel when you wanted to be brave and courageous but were unable to do so?

13. What part do you think bravery played in your early girlhood and how do you think it shaped and molded your life?

14. When your bravery failed you, what happened and how did you feel?

15. How did being brave change things for the better?

After you complete this exercise, review it thoroughly. Do you notice any recurring themes or patterns that seem to jump out at you? In what ways do these patterns affect your present beliefs, attitudes, and feelings about yourself and others?

Research Your Roots and Early Biography

One of the best ways to explore your bravery is by reconstructing your early biography. Begin by consulting with family members and relatives about their memories of you as a little girl and a preadolescent. Ask your immediate family members, their friends, anyone who knew you when you were younger to provide you with a thumbnail sketch of their memories of you. Were you a bold little tyke? Were you fresh? Maybe you were a "wise ass"? Or shy? Were you quiet? Adventuresome?

Ask your family and relatives to provide you with feedback. They can do this verbally or on paper, it doesn't matter. Have them free-associate first and then provide you with their more in-depth observations. When you have collected several of these impressions, compare them with each other and with your own memories. Do they jibe?

Write up your girlhood biography based on these impressions and embellish them with your own memories of the way you were. In other words, write a composite story of your girlhood told from your point of view and theirs. Free write it: Don't worry about the grammar or style. Let your family's input trigger your thoughts.

Reading through the biography you write will help you to think about and view your history in new ways and, at certain points, will trigger and evoke a variety of emotions. Monitor these flashpoints. What are you feeling as you read each part? A strong reaction signals a significant problem or unresolved issue. Are you still struggling with particular memories or events?

Brave Women in Your History

Another entry into your bravery is to connect with the brave women in your family of origin: your mother, your grandmother, great aunts, living or dead. The best way to research your brave roots is to ask family members and explore the Internet. There are software programs to facilitate your search, and books and guides to aid you in the process.

Libby: A Brave New Path

Mary has often been told she is very much like her grandmother on her mother's side. Her name was Elizabeth, but everyone called her Libby, and she died eight months before Mary was born.

Libby's bravery continues to resonate with the next generations. She was born and raised an Irish Catholic. Even at the end of the last century, she rejected the prescription that women shouldn't work, and she studied typing in a pool of young men. After graduation, she got herself a job as a secretary, known as a "typewriter" at that time, and went to work in a large lye- and soap-making factory owned and run by a wealthy Jewish family. Even though she had many attractive marriage offers from eligible Catholic bachelors, she fell in love with one of the Jewish sons of the factory owner.

Libby loved the man, her husband of thirty-two years, so profoundly that she abandoned her mother's house in 1899 and, once excommunicated, never looked back on her people, her religion, or her destiny at birth. Instead she eloped, knowing that her future husband had risked his fortune by marrying what his parents called a "shiksa," or a non-Jewish girl. They lived as exiles from both of their families, until she took Hebrew lessons in secret and contrived to meet up with her in-laws with her baby, Samuel, in a carriage. There was a huge reconciliation. Elizabeth went on to become one of the wealthiest matrons in her community, and when her less fortunate relatives appeared at her doorstep, she never turned them away.

Inspired by Roots of Bravery

Researching your roots, finding out about the members of your family, alive or deceased, will give you a context for your bravery and make you feel part of the family history and traditions. Delia, one of the women interviewed for this book, described how she had traced her great-grandmother's history and learned that her relative had run away from a Southern plantation where she was a slave and escaped up north to Troy, New York, via the Underground Railroad. Empowered by this piece of personal history that "tipped the scale for her," Delia made the decision to join the Peace Corps, a longtime dream of hers that she had hesitated to pursue until inspired by her ancestor's bravery.

Leah: A Brave New Path

Leah's girlhood reads like an inspirational novel. She grew up in a small midwestern town, the daughter of Orthodox Jewish Russian immigrants who couldn't write or speak any English. Today, Leah is a literature professor known around the world for her scholarship. Remembering her roots—where she came from—inspires Leah when she requires courage.

From birth, Leah had a disability that first manifested itself when she started to walk and became more pronounced in grade school. Recreation class was particularly painful, especially because she was always picked last to be on a team. To compensate, Leah developed the habit of thinking fast and was able to verbalize what others' were thinking; a great speller, she was picked first for the spelling bee.

She has a memory of walking home from grade school and being pelted with snowballs. They had rocks in them and stung her legs, creating large red welts that her mother patted with a soothing astringent. "The Catholic kids didn't know what a Jew was; a Jew to them was someone who walked funny." Leah laughed and joked.

Leah's mother, who had the same disability as three of her children, was particularly overprotective of her daughter, the youngest of five children, and guilty about transmitting this genetic makeup. When her mother said you can't do this or that, Leah defied her, "Yes I can, Ma, I can!" Her father believed in her and encouraged her to do anything she wanted. To this day, when someone tells Leah she can't do something, she's defiant, motivated to prove them wrong.

Leah departed her girlhood and went on to excel in high school and college, taught high school, received her Ph.D., and became a professor of English. She is a scholar and author, a playwright with nine produced plays, and has been happily married to the same man for thirty-five years. "There is an indefatigable force inside me," she says. The bravest thing she has ever done? She traveled on an extended Eastern Europe tour by herself. "I flew on a German airline and a tired Arab man sat next to me and even put his head on my shoulder during the flight."

The Genderless Woman

Gene N. Landrum (1999), in his book *Eight Keys to Greatness: How to Unlock Your Hidden Potential*, studies and profiles exceptional women and men who have changed the world. He found that one of the key characteristics of greatness is the ability of both sexes to "tap into their syzygy" or "flip-flop between different dimensions of personality, gender, and even ideologies" (243).

According to Landrum, *syzygy* describes a natural phenomenon when all the planets are lined up. Transpose this occurrence to people or aesthetics, and you produce the Asian effect of yin and yang, the totality and balance of life; Carl Jung's personality psychology; and the work of Mihalyi Csikszentmihalyi, of the University of Chicago, who postulated that "the most creative individuals escape rigid gender stereotyping and tend to androgyny" (245).

In girlhood, the gender dimensions of our personalities are more dual and synthesized. Of course, these dualities have nothing to do with whether someone is masculine or feminine in appearance or orientation. In fact, men and women who naturally "gender-bend" and who tap into all aspects of their personalities are powerful magnets for the opposite sex. Celebrities, rock stars, famous label designers, and more capitalize on these ambiguities and have been on the cutting edge with this concept for at least two decades.

Women from Catherine the Great to the great Katherine Hepburn, who have lived on their own terms, are bold, audacious, feminine, complex, open, soft, poetic, and gutsy all at once. They felt entitled to say or do anything they chose and have defied the impositions of gender stereotypes and roles. Some of the most interesting and creative men transcend gender, refusing to be bound by exaggerated and cumbersome stereotypes.

Channeling Eleanor

Two women who exemplify gender-transcending bravery are Eleanor Roosevelt and Hillary Rodham Clinton. Neither woman limited herself to conventional boundaries and the confines of prescribed roles. Both first ladies expressed their human potential and individual aspirations, despite raised eyebrows and widespread censure.

It has been widely reported that when faced with a challenge, now Senator but then First Lady Hillary Rodham Clinton would "channel" Eleanor Roosevelt for inspiration and guidance. "What would Eleanor do in my situation?" Hillary would ask herself when under fire or faced with her husband's infidelity and the many other challenges of living in the White House. She strongly identified with President Franklin Delano Roosevelt's wife, that brave, controversial woman who stepped out of several prescribed roles in the Thirties and Forties. Of course, it's one thing to channel and identify with some great historic figure, and another to live up to their standards.

Both Hillary Rodham Clinton and Eleanor Roosevelt are controversial figures. Each woman provokes ardent emotions from all sides of the political fence. Both had strong convictions and opinions. They took stands on the thorniest issues of the day, and they stepped out of their prescribed roles as wives, mothers, and first ladies. Looking at Hillary and Eleanor more closely, at a deeper, more archetypal level, it seems these women pushed people's buttons because of their ability to migrate across personality boundaries, to cross gender limitations, role-specific behavior, and ideological borders. In the Thirties, Forties, and Fifties, Eleanor even transgressed sexual parameters.

A Quintessentially Brave Woman

In every sense, Eleanor Roosevelt was the "total woman" of her time. "Every woman in public life needs to develop skin as tough as a rhinoceros hide." These words from Eleanor Roosevelt would naturally reverberate years later with Hillary Rodham Clinton. Eleanor's words, personal qualities, and inspirational history are standards any woman can admire. Eleanor fought shyness and fears all her life, yet became one of the most public figures of the twentieth century. She overcame an unhappy childhood, the tyranny of a domineering mother-in-law, the conventions of social class, her husband's infidelity, and what she called her "Griselda moods," extended depressive episodes before the age of antidepressants.

Eleanor Roosevelt exemplifies the woman whose past didn't determine her future. Born into one of the country's most prominent families, she was a socialite "ugly duckling." Her mother constantly conveyed her disappointment to her daughter that she was not a great beauty. The father she worshipped and adored proved to be unreliable and selfish, with a chronic drinking problem. Her marriage to her distant cousin Franklin didn't assuage her insecurities and perpetuated her unliberated roles.

During and after World War I, Eleanor cast off the roles of mother, society matron, even wife. She entered into politics, championing the rights of the poor, the mentally disabled, interred and buried Japanese-Americans, and women workers; she engineered her husband's ascent to the White House, insisting that his bout with polio that had left him wheelchair bound would not cripple his national ambitions.

One of Eleanor Roosevelt's most famous brave acts was to arrange for the soprano Marian Anderson to give a public concert on the steps of the Lincoln Memorial after the Daughters of the American Revolution (DAR) refused to allow Anderson to perform at Constitution Hall because she was black. The poet Archibald MacLeish dubbed Eleanor Roosevelt "the conscience of the nation" when she served as a U.N. ambassador advocating for global human rights.

Eleanor contended with comments about her "overreaching" role as first lady and the presence of another woman in her husband's life. Her heartbreak on learning about Franklin's affair with Lucy was incalculable and carried on until his death when, after thinking the affair was over, Eleanor found out that her own daughter, Anna, had arranged for a deathbed rendezvous between Lucy and Franklin. Eleanor's own love life was risqué and unique even by twenty-first century standards.

Although plain and shy, Eleanor Roosevelt's presence, charisma, and character attracted both sexes from women like Associated Press reporter Lorena Hickock (Eleanor's traveling companion and possible lover) to the aristocratic Franklin to Earl Miller, the dashing New York State trooper assigned to be Eleanor's bodyguard.

The First Doll

The largest babushka doll appears whole and complete, yet her exterior conceals vast worlds inside her. Her smiling face tells only part of her story, and, like your personal biography, it is only an introduction to what's really going on inside. You, too, are made up of inner shells—webs and networks of memories, hurts, pains, history, desires, fears, emotional baggage, and more—that determine how you think, why you experience the world in certain ways, and how brave you are willing to be.

As you complete the exercises throughout the book, you will experience more of your own bravery as you begin revealing and exfoliating the multiple layers of your own babushka qualities. You will reflect on what it means for you to be a brave woman, and what bravery does to enrich and expand your life. You will look closely at the choices you've made and discover how your bravery affects everything. As you progress through the coming chapters, you will gain a clearer picture of the goals and map you have charted for yourself, and you will learn what—if anything—needs to be discarded and replaced to reflect the brave new you.

Chapter 2

Let Go of Your Past, Seize Your Future

Break Free of the Matrix and Reinvent Yourself

*I am not waiting around for anyone from above
to give me the signal. We just have to step
forward with our hearts and act.*

—Natalie Goldberg

The second dynamic strategy for becoming a brave woman is to realize that you can dramatically change your life and your future by truly reinventing yourself. You're reminded in this chapter that your life is not a set of fixed circumstances and you *can* change. You have choices; you're not on autopilot. You always have control of the instruments of your own plane. This chapter reacquaints you with how to change direction and modify your flight plan, as your situation requires.

The Red Pill and the Blue Pill

One of the most popular movies of the recent past was *The Matrix* (Wachowski Bros. 1999), a high-tech, futuristic film that closely resembles Alice's adventures in Wonderland. The film's premise is that human beings live in a "virtual world," a simulated matrix, and don't know it. They go about their "real world" activities—work, school, play, and lovemaking—unaware that their world actually is synthetic: a programmed virtual existence that hides the truth about their predicament and true condition. Only a select few have moved between the worlds and possess knowledge about their true reality.

Neo, the film's hero and "the One" who can pierce through life's illusions and eventually destroy the matrix, lands, like Alice in Wonderland, into the real world where he must retrain his mind and body for the ultimate challenge. Neo has the possibility to fulfill his destiny and discover the truth about himself, his full potential, his history, his people, and his future. But, first, he must convince himself that he is capable of overcoming formidable odds and that he is "the One" in control of his own destiny, and ultimately, the human race.

To find his life's mission, Neo must choose between swallowing a red pill or a blue pill. "Take the blue pill and the story ends," says Morpheus, his mentor and guide. "You wake up in your bed and believe whatever you want to believe. You take the red pill and you stay in Wonderland, and I show you how deep the rabbit hole goes. Remember all I am offering is the truth—nothing more." Neo can either stay in Wonderland, the real world outside the matrix, and learn the truth about himself and the world, or he can continue to remain in his pseudo-reality without being aware of his greatness.

Consciously Choose Bravery

Many of you, either deliberately or unknowingly, choose to swallow the blue pill and live in the world of the matrix where everything that you see, touch, hear, and feel seems real to your senses, but, in fact, is filled with illusions and fictions created by you and for you. Many women may fear to see things as they are, so they discard the red pill and hide the truth from themselves.

One of the greatest difficulties in expressing women's bravery is discovering how other people's "best intentions" can actually be harmful—especially if you don't know yourself well, or if you fail to take other people's motivations and hidden agendas into account. Many people in your life want you to be successful, happy, and fulfilled, to see your dreams turn into reality. They take pleasure in your triumphs over adversity and applaud your achievements. They welcome and respect the improvements in your life, your individual growth, and appreciate the courage that this work demands.

As you express the courage to better understand yourself and to truly create a more abundant and rewarding life, however, there are those close to you—your partners, family members, friends, coworkers—who, at times, will find it difficult to understand, let alone accept, that you are changing and that you are "different." When this happens, their bewilderment, upset, and even anger may lead them to criticize you. They begin to wonder where the "other person" whom they used to know has gone.

It is critical at this juncture that your bravery not desert you. You might feel that your changes are "wrong," that you're letting people down and hurting them by your emboldened acts of courageous self-interest. You might begin to experience guilt and remorse for daring to make demands of others, or for experimenting, trying to do things differently, shaking up your routines.

"Who am I to think that things can be different?" you might ask yourself. At this point, the old myths about your life may surface and reactivate. The myth that your past equals your future tries to reassert itself. Don't let it—swallow the red pill.

Diane: A Brave New Path

"Why can't I swallow the red pill?" asks Diane, an attractive household worker. At age forty-seven, Diane would like to start her own catering business and extricate herself from a painful marriage, but she is too frightened to do either.

"When I was twelve," Diane remembers, "I wasn't afraid of anything. I wasn't afraid to make choices or to stand up for what I believed in. I was a spunky little kid who said what I felt to anybody." Those outside her immediate family viewed her as "fresh" and too independent for her own good. Diane's parents encouraged her to follow the paths of her childhood dreams. They coached her to work hard, be fair to others, and make something of herself.

At one point Diane dreamed of being a stewardess; at another, she wanted to build a truck for her father, who had a landscaping and snowplowing business. She even wanted to be an FBI agent—to follow people around and catch them in the acts of spying and espionage.

Everything changed when Diana turned sixteen. Her mother had a heart attack, her father became ill, and her sisters married and moved away. Not only did she give up on those dreams and her ambitions, but Diane also lost her nerve. Her self-talk went something like this: "It's easier to make the same mistakes over and over again. At least I know the outcomes and how to deal with them. I've been there, done that, many times before." Diane, like many women, felt safe, secure, and accustomed to her unhappiness, painful as it was. She simply "puts up with life" instead of exploring and discovering the abundance of life's options and possibilities.

Breaking Free of "The Chipped Plate" Syndrome

A. Manette Ansay's best-selling novel *Vinegar Hill* (1999) begins, "In the gray light of the kitchen, Ellen sets the table for supper keeping the chipped plate for herself." This opening line captures many women's tendency—you might even call it an automatic reflex—to sacrifice their needs and pleasures to benefit others. Women have routinely "set the table" and made life beautiful for everyone but them. In "keeping the chipped plate for herself," Ellen typifies the common female phenomenon of negating one's own dreams while facilitating others'.

Is Ellen's pattern of behavior familiar? Do you fantasize about what your life could be like instead of treating yourself and savoring the best life has to serve up on the finest damask china? Women have tended historically to feel less entitled to their due and unintentionally settle for second best. Somewhere in the depths of their being there may be a voice that says, "My dreams are impractical or not important," or "I could never do that," or " That's impossible." Many women remain in the background, untested, and continue to pave the way for their partners, children, and bosses to get ahead.

For the Sake of Others

Julie, a Detroit-based stock broker, plays doubles tennis early in the morning with a group of professional women before they go to work. One day her tennis partner, Myrna, a top official and physician with a state health department, returned a serve, ripping a brilliant passing shot down the alley past their opponent. The opponent could only whiff at the ball as it speeded past her. "Oh, I'm really sorry," Myrna apologized. "I should never do that. That wasn't nice."

Can you imagine a man apologizing for being competent or excelling at something, especially a sport? Unfortunately, it's more common for a woman to play down her intelligence, suppress her natural strengths and powers, and place others' sense of security and well-being before her own. The idea of planning the future without a safety net and taking the significant and important risks to guarantee those outcomes causes many women to lose heart and stop themselves in their tracks. Their best-laid plans jettisoned, they derail their aspirations, and never venture forth. They hear and remember others' messages—what they were like as children, and how they should be as adults.

Myrna had a tendency to often sacrifice herself for the sake of others' needs. She remembers being offered a top post at the U.S. Department of Health and Human Services during the early years of the Clinton administration. She turned it down, however, because she didn't want to break up her family. Ironically, a year later she was divorced. To this day, she regrets not having taken the major risk to more fully explore a position that appeared—at least on the surface—to be her "dream job."

The expectations placed on women and the pressures to conform are also powerful forces in shaping how you view what you can do, how you should be, and how you should act.

A challenge for all women to decide: Are you willing to keep taking and settling for "the chipped plate" or are you ready to become the brave woman you were meant to be?

Crack Open the First Doll

You have a choice. You can ingest blue pills that are plentiful and easy to swallow. Or you can dare to swallow the red pill, buckle your seat belt, brace yourself for the ride, and follow the white rabbit toward the adventure of a lifetime. And it doesn't matter where you are right now.

Brave women pick the red pill to get a clearer picture about themselves, the world they inhabit, and the journey that lies before them. They burrow in the rabbit hole as deep as it goes and for as long as it takes. They accept and even enjoy the way it twists and turns, tumble into the hidden passages, and take responsibility for the fact that perhaps they have been living in a less than genuine manner.

The Red Pill Test

Please read the following questions and answer "yes" or "no" to each one.

1. Have you been putting a positive spin on a bad situation, a friendship, a relationship, or a marriage?

2. Do you sugarcoat problems and make "nice nice" in an attempt to make them evaporate?

3. Do you let others take advantage of you or not even let yourself entertain the possibility that others have an agenda?

4. Do you say "yes" when you really mean to say "no"?

5. Do you escape from who you really are inside with busyness, others' interruptions, and constant companionship—anything to avoid facing yourself?

6. Do you make a habit of acting passive or overly aggressive or a combination of the two?

7. Are you living with false and unrealistic expectations about other people's behavior and the disappointment that comes from this?

8. Do you allow fear to dictate your choices and stop you from pursuing your goals and ambitions?

Living the Truth

If you responded "yes" to any of the eight questions above, there's a good chance that you need to work on your bravery to live a more authentic life. In one sense, all of these questions and answers relate to your ability to tell the truth. Living bravely is living honestly. Telling the "naked truth" means disarming yourself and losing many of your defenses. If you don't tell yourself the truth, you can never move on.

"Putting a spin on" or rationalizing a bad situation or relationship postpones the inevitable and makes it even more difficult to come to terms with it in the long run. Realize it takes time to work through sticky situations and even break them off if necessary. Add up the pluses and minuses. Does the upside outweigh the downside of your situation?

Similarly, seeing others as you want or expect them to be leaves you vulnerable and ripe for disappointment. Other people are not a mirror image of you. They have different ideas, backgrounds, goals, motivations, and agendas. Seeing others as they are is difficult and sometimes painful. Not seeing others as they are is even more distressing: the result is that others may take advantage of you and suck your vitality and energy.

The best way to see others more clearly is to honestly look at yourself. Seeing yourself with more clarity leaves you with fewer defenses; you will have less need to distort your perceptions or to distance how you see other people.

Saying "yes" when you really mean "no" is a prescription for stockpiling anger in your system. Stockpiled anger can turn into chronic rage or lead to depression. Being honest and saying what you mean prevents all these conditions.

The way to become aware if you are always agreeable and automatically say "yes" even if you mean "no" is to monitor what you're feeling *before* you say "yes." Practice saying "no" and *afterward* determine what your feelings are.

If you use overbusyness to block the truth from yourself, you are depriving yourself of the great pleasure of knowing who you are. External noise in all forms obstructs the passageways to your inner being. It is only in the stillness that you can hear your inner voice that speaks its genuine truth to you. In chapter 12, you will learn how to turn off the noise and hear the whisperings of your brave, essential self.

Finally, allowing fear to dictate your choices cripples your ambitions and puts up a roadblock between you and your dreams. Fear is your ally, not an enemy. As you will learn in chapter 5, the brave new you will know how to use fear for empowerment.

Voyages of Self-Discovery

Journeys into the matrix, or Oz, or Wonderland, are actually metaphors for voyages of self-discovery.

Following the White Rabbit

The white rabbit may lead Alice through a tangled wonderland of mad hatters and a queen of hearts, yet any woman, young, old, or in-between, can look at the illogical and topsy-turvy nature of her reality and change course by throwing out her outmoded maps. With a rejuvenated determination and new understanding of herself and her circumstances, she can set a new course for her life, making adjustments and changes based on the "greater truth" of her life situation.

Alice slowly gains the upper hand during her unusual adventures and emerges from her dream able to assert her strength of character and determination as she gains mastery of the brave woman inside. Remember, you too have that brave woman in you.

A Journey to Oz

In the Wizard of Oz, Dorothy tumbles into Munchkinland and bravely follows the yellow brick road to the Emerald City. Once there, she confronts her everyday problems disguised as a wicked witch and a phony wizard. She thinks other people have the answers for her life, hence the phony wizard, and that she is powerless to get out of Oz and the clutches of her enemies. Her companions, the scarecrow, the tin man, and the lion, represent the three main potentialities of all brave women—her brain, her heart, and her bravery. Dorothy learns to rely on these inner resources with increasing confidence. She discovers that what she thought she was missing was inside her all along.

Brainpower

The challenges within this novel environment compel Dorothy to express her creative abilities and reasoning powers. She uses her *brainpower* to maneuver around the obstacles and difficulties that waylay her on the journey through Oz. Her increasing confidence in her own judgment allows her to make greater sense of things.

Empathetic Distance

Dorothy's heart is open to the plight of her three stalwarts, and her compassion for them is the fuel that drives her bravery. She expresses her rich emotional life through her passionate commitment to right the injustices done to her friends. She keeps an *empathetic distance* from her companions, caring deeply for their plight, giving them direction that will solve their problems, and advocating for them with the Wizard. But she doesn't get so engrossed by her friends' problems that she becomes embedded in them to her own exclusion and detriment.

Confronting Authority

Finally Dorothy exhibits courage—the willingness to put herself on the line for her beliefs and values, and to *confront authority* in the guise of the puffed-up Wizard who hides behind an empty title and unsubstantiated power. When she returns home to Kansas, Dorothy is transformed. She is more confident, braver, and wiser. And, we suspect, a more empowered person.

You Can Change Your Life

Surprising as it may seem, one momentous act of bravery can change your life and take you to a new plateau of understanding and self-empowerment. Such acts of bravery include:

- Leaving someone who is not good for you, despite the fact that you love him.

- Coming out of the closet about your sexual identity.
- Donating an organ.

More usual are the brave incremental steps we take to "test the waters" of the unknown and the new. For example:

- Saying "no" to someone's request.
- Speaking up against someone's insensitive remark.
- Deciding to travel on your own.
- Making it clear that you disapprove of someone's behavior.

With each courageous act, you gain the confidence to take stronger and more determined steps, which invigorate your bravery along the way. It's a matter of getting into that "new groove."

In the following story, Leticia turned her life around by first confronting and then changing the rules of her abusive relationship with her brother. This victory sparked her long-dormant bravery—fueling her passion and equipping her with the determination to superimpose a new blueprint for her life over one that had previously brought only unhappiness and despair.

Leticia: A Brave New Path

Leticia is studying to be a civil rights' attorney. After graduation from law school, she plans to help "my people" as she calls them—Mexican migrant workers and others who can't afford the services of an attorney. Ironically this thirty-two-year-old woman grew up ashamed of herself and her family, as well as her Mexican heritage and its patriarchal traditions.

"My mother always dressed us up to look our best. Even though our household was a living hell, she had to make it look like we were the perfect family," says Leticia. "I learned very early on that girls had certain duties and boys had the privileges. My brothers could enjoy their adolescence. I was expected to have the house cleaned by 3:30 P.M. when my mother came home from work. I walked on eggshells all the time, fearing the appearance of my father's leather belt, which my mother would whack me with on the back of my hands."

At those times, Leticia would retreat to her room, hide under the bed, and test how little she meant to her family by determining how long it took for them to notice she had "disappeared." Her parents insisted she and her brothers attend church every Sunday where Leticia would question how God had allowed all this to happen to her.

As she grew older, Leticia's resentment intensified; her mother's abuse and alcoholic rages, and her two brothers' violent behavior toward her continued to escalate. Eventually, Leticia turned to alcohol and drugs to escape the abuse and deaden the pain of her own self-hatred.

To Leticia's dismay, drugs and alcohol didn't better her situation. Finally, in total despair and near ruin, Leticia realized that she had little time to straighten out her life. She knew that to continue on this path meant certain death. If not a physical death, it would surely be the death of her soul.

A Turning Point of Bravery

Three years ago, just hours after her father's funeral, Leticia discovered the brave woman inside herself. Sitting with her older brother, comforting him on their mutual loss, she firmly told him: "I forgive you for what you've done to me for all these years, but I want you to know that as long as you continue to abuse and insult me, there is no longer any room for you in my life." Her priest and confidante, who was in the room consoling the family, turned around and said, "I'm so proud of you. You have grown so much."

"I felt like Popeye after he ate a can of spinach," Leticia says about her feelings at the time. That was the turning point. From then on Leticia stood up for herself and fought for her rights and for the recognition, if not respect, of her family members. She set strong limits with those who had previously showed callous disregard for her thoughts and feelings.

This brave new woman refused to be verbally and physically abused, or to be manipulated or exploited. In effect, she put up a "do not trespass" sign with a warning that those who did would do so at their own peril. This was one of the most liberating experiences of her life; it provided her the confidence to pursue her life dreams, which were now palpable and real to her, and not merely the fantasies of a once fearful woman.

Leticia's newfound liberation of self and spirit fueled her motivation to reconstruct the cultural identity she had loathed and hidden from herself for so many years. She realized that her ethic roots were part of her identity and not to be confused with the suffering and belittlement that she had experienced at the hands of her brothers and parents.

At college, Leticia celebrated the rich mythological and life-enhancing aspects of her native cultural heritage, but she decided to distance herself from those ideas and traditions with which she disagreed. When she imagines her spiritual self these days, Leticia closes her eyes and sees a "huge Aztec woman with beautiful copper skin and jet-black hair wearing a silver headdress made of pink, blue, and yellow feathers."

Because of her bravery, Leticia experienced a shift in her values. Moving on with her life caused her to rearrange her priorities. "I am proud of who I am; I come first now, then my children, my relationship, my mother, my higher power. My partner can leave any day. I hope he won't, but if he does, I will survive and know that this too shall pass, and my children and I will be happy and loving."

Taking Inventory

Once found, the brave woman inside you wears down your excuses for keeping things the same. She directs you to the truth of what you're living and provides you the opportunity for choice, direction, and fulfillment in your life. Her opposite, cowardice, is born of fear: the fear of thinking for yourself; the fear of doing for yourself; and the fear of risking your security for something better. This is why the brave woman exhibits boldness in her actions and achieves the kind of personal satisfaction that other women can only envy.

The courage to face the truth of your life is what sets you free; it allows you to soar to unimaginable and sometimes dizzying heights. The truth is that your life is short, yet in this fleeting period of time allotted to you, it behooves you to make your mark in this world, to fashion a masterpiece of your life. Be an example for other women to follow. Yes, you can serve as that model—it's the best way to live; it is the only way to live.

It can be most difficult to actually think about what you are doing: Are you making excuses, creating rationales, gossiping, status-seeking, competing, seeking revenge, muddying other peoples' lives, etc.? Are you participating in any activity that diminishes the quality of your life? To really think about these habits, stop what you're doing, sit alone with yourself, and allow your still, inner voice to break through.

Ask Yourself These Questions

- Are you afraid to speak your mind for fear of criticism or being abandoned?
- Do you have a hard time standing up for your rights?
- Do you follow the lead of others rather than your own?
- Are you so overwhelmed by fear that it prevents you from being all that you can be?
- Do you make excuses for your unhappiness?

It's time to take an inventory of what you do, why you do it, and why you persist in doing things in the same old way even though it is no longer helpful or meaningful to your life. Don't sacrifice substance and meaning for responsibility and obligation as if they were mutually exclusive, when in fact they are not.

This type of questioning and exploration allows the courage and bravery within you to shape and mold the person you truly want to become. Your mission is to create a life of meaning, substance, and authenticity. So that, in the end, when you look back, you can smile and know you have done your best and given it your all, with no regrets, and having never to lament lost opportunities.

A Personal History Lesson

Most people embellish their memory banks with events, ideas, and beliefs to align themselves with how they *want* to feel. As a result, people revise, distort, camouflage, minimize, maximize, catastrophize, and, to a degree, fabricate what's happened to them. Your personal history distortions, large or small, measure the extent to which you have defended yourself from life's vicissitudes. Virtually everyone engages in revisionist history as a way of dealing with the slights, hurt, and pain, or the happiness, joy, and mixed feelings attached to significant and pivotal life events. How you dealt with your feelings during those times shaped your version of the truth.

Have you heard the adage that "comedy equals tragedy plus time"? The equation comes from Woody Allen's film *Crimes and Misdemeanors* (1989). In other words, something dreadful happens and, at the time, we think it's a disaster. For example, you aren't accepted into a certain college or graduate school, you don't get that job, or that part, or that promotion, you end a romantic relationship, or your soul mate finds another. Five years later, you often laugh at the same "tragedy" and marvel at the ironic outcome of those same situations. The graduate school you originally wanted discontinued its doctoral program the following year. What did you ever see in that creepy guy, anyway? Not getting that part allowed you to try out for the sitcom you are in right now. Tragedy plus time equals comedy.

Think of two or three distant "tragedies" in your life. Are they still tragic or are they some of the best things that ever happened to you?

Welcome to the Fun House:
An Exercise

As you look at your past, you must be careful not to exaggerate what you perceive to be your accomplishments. You are especially vulnerable to peering at yourself through "rose-colored glasses" when you feel less than good about yourself. Adding to the problem of seeing past events accurately is that your memories change with time as one memory superimposes itself on another. Your memories are akin to your image reshaped and contorted in a fun-house mirror. You know what you are looking at, but what peers back is twisted and contorted, not a true representation.

As you read the questions below, it is important that you write what comes immediately to your mind. Don't judge, criticize, or censor your thoughts and observations. Remember, judging and censoring what comes to your awareness will distort, repress, and remove memories, beliefs, and attitudes that may be of critical importance to the way you feel about yourself and the way you conduct your life.

- My earliest memory is:

- My most painful memory is the time when:

- The most difficult period I've ever had was:

- My greatest failure was the time I:

- The words I would use to characterize my past are:

- Our household at holidays was:

- The most unusual aspect of my past is:

- The person who undermined me the most was:

- I am most ashamed about the time I:

- The most traumatic event or series of events I've gone through are:

- In our family, I was always considered the:

- My favorite relative growing up was:

- If I wrote a sitcom about my family it would be:

- My brother(s) and/or sister(s) used to:

- I felt most sexy and attractive when:

- I am haunted by the memory of:

As you review the experiences of your life, make a note of what was the happiest and most fulfilling. Review the periods of your life that were the saddest and most difficult. How did this affect you then? In what ways do you think it's affecting you now? How do you think it will continue to affect you in the future? Do your answers surprise you?

Whether you valiantly struggle to repress, control, or fully experience your feelings determines the degree to which you walk with clarity in your life or distort and falsify past events. Embracing your emotions without judging them—whether they are pleasant or difficult—yields the unblemished truth about yourself and your circumstances, and allows you to ponder the true essence of who you are and what you've experienced.

Chapter 3

Dump False Beliefs That Limit You

When I ran for a seat in the U.S. Senate, I was considered a nobody. I didn't have a long political background. I didn't come from a family of wealth. I didn't come as an insider Democrat who had risen up through the ranks. I was a common person. I was a woman.

—Senator Patty Murray

Dynamic strategy No. 3 is to become sensitive to your unique experiences as a woman and to understand the cultural forces that mold your way of thinking, the values most important to you, your upbringing as a girl, and why you behave in certain ways. You will become aware of common misconceptions and myths that may shape your reality and limit your opportunities, your self-expression, and damage your self-worth. You will learn not to fall victim to these cultural myths of desirability and instead strike a healthy balance between your appearance, your character, and your intelligence.

Gender Based Stereotypes

Some of the most ubiquitous stereotypes that affect a woman's preferences, career choices, lifestyle, and more are gender-based. The brave woman ignores stereotypes and listens to herself when choosing how to live and whom to love. She doesn't see status and power in terms of gender, and she is comfortable with her ability to influence others.

Sex Appeal

The sex appeal of that mind of hers was truly captivating.

—Jane Howard speaking
about Margaret Mead

One of the stronger gender-based stereotypes that continues to persist has to do with sex appeal. Many people have been conditioned to think of sex appeal as emanating from outer garments or a woman's body—wearing slinky, tight clothes, mile-high heels, performing sexual acrobatics, and providing unusual pleasures. The irony is that true sex appeal originates from inside you where a woman projects an aura of self-possession and personal power.

Status, energy, charisma, a lively mind, confidence, and intelligence also enhance a woman's allure and desirability. Add to these being a "straight shooter," living up to the standards that you've set for yourself, and being authentic and real.

Sex appeal isn't just another good-looking body: it's going after what you want and speaking your mind—that's sexy. Eighteenth century novelist Jane Austen created heroines with this kind of sexual charisma. Austen's heroines in books like *Emma* (1816) or *Sense and Sensibility* (1811), portrayed most recently in film adaptations by Gwyneth Paltrow and Emma Thompson, win over the men they love with bravery and self-assurance rather than seduction or entrapment.

Sex appeal commonly is associated with youth. The youth-obsessed American culture, films, magazines, and the media endorse the appeal of young and very thin women and continually re-enforce unrealistic ideals and beauty images that leave most women out of the running. The culture's mindset induces women to fear aging and to worry about not being youthful and attractive to their mate. Women in epidemic proportions hate their bodies—no matter what they do, they don't believe they look good enough.

A woman is truly brave who can withstand these cultural assaults and the not-so-subtle messages that bombard women every day. The main message: You are not acceptable as you are, and you must change your body to feel good about yourself or to attract a desirable mate or to keep the one you have.

Is it any wonder that a woman gets down on herself as she struggles in vain to reach these unreal, airbrushed images of perfection? Women fall victim to the constant blitz and propaganda designed to make them buy magazines and spend money on beauty and diets that will eventually demoralize and defeat them over and over again. Society's defects somehow get translated into women's flaws.

What about men? Men aren't faced with the same kind of pressures that women experience. Although there has been a growing trend for men to pursue the similar "beauty myth" track that women do, it is eclipsed by the sheer volume of messages that women receive about their "unacceptable" selves.

The Pink and Blue Blanket

Certain expectations and stereotypes are commonly attached to both sexes. Interestingly, these gender-based assumptions begin when most of us are too young even to remember. The following "experiment" illustrates this poignant truth.

After their baby boy was born, Jean and Donald, a couple of psychologists, held two open houses to mark the blessed occasion for family and friends. The invitation read: "Please come celebrate the birth of our first child." For the first party, when Sam was six weeks old, they dressed him in pink and introduced him to his first batch of admirers. "What an adorable little Sam," they said. "She's so feminine and fragile—look at those long eyelashes. She'll be a heartbreaker and make some man a wonderful wife some day." Two weeks later, his parents tucked Sam into a blue receiving blanket and showed him off again to other friends and neighbors. "What a husky kid," they remarked. "Look at those chubby little arms. He's got the makings of a fullback."

Their experiment underlines the arbitrary nature of gender and how gender identity shifts with an individual's perception. Depending on the blanket color or "packaging" one sees, girl babies and boy babies are approached and handled differently.

Closing the Gender Gap

Your views and beliefs about what it is to be a "woman" or a "man" are based on what you've seen, what you've been told, and what you've read and learned. Your socialization and beliefs regarding gender issues and differences cause you to experience a "selective perception" of characteristic male and female behaviors and what is acceptable for each sex. In other words, you may choose to see certain characteristics and tend to ignore others to fit the views that you have about men and women.

You may believe that men behave and think in certain ways, and that women are supposed to think and behave in other ways. When men and women don't fit that framework, the tendency is to pigeonhole, and see them as either lacking femininity or masculinity. Or perhaps you see them as overreaching—trying to be something they aren't—or that they have some kind of problem, or that they're trying to be "different" than that which their gender requires of them. The woman who postpones marriage or never marries, the man who chooses to remain single, the childless couple, the diplomat who spends Christmas with the troops overseas rather than with her daughter's family are all examples of some people's notions of gender-based nonconformance.

When Marlene and Paul had been married for about six years, they began to notice that their behaviors greatly reversed traditional gender roles and stereotypes. Paul seemed to be the one who insists on open and direct communication about relationship issues and problems—"laying it all out on the table." He was the one who urges them both to sit down and talk out their concerns; Marlene clams up and is more reticent, holding back, like a "typical male," from dealing with feelings and emotional issues. Conversely, Marlene is the sports' fan. Although Paul can remember who hit how many home runs in a certain year, when there's a significant sports' event, Marlene is the one glued to the television set. While some differences may reflect their professional training, both believe that adhering to prepackaged gender roles and stereotyped behavior curtails spontaneity and makes for a less vital and creative relationship.

The beliefs you hold about gender differences profoundly affect your choices: who you are, what you want to be, and what you want to do. They influence how you act, what books, films, sports, and music you should like and dislike, what you think you are capable of doing or not doing, and more.

You need to look at and examine your beliefs about men and women to release yourself from ideas that limit the expression of your bravery. It's imperative that you overcome gender obstacles and other people's expectations based strictly on whether you are a woman or a man. Gender differences and externally imposed roles do not dictate a brave woman's choices in life, what she can or cannot do, or how she thinks about and relates to the world.

Test Your Gender Attitudes: An Exercise

First, make a list of fifteen characteristics that you associate more with women than with men. Then make a list of fifteen characteristics that you associate with men more than women. At the end of each characteristic, assign it a number from one to five: five indicates an outstanding and very admirable trait, one indicates a poor characteristic that is detrimental and unhelpful, and three is neutral, not necessarily a poor quality to have, but not necessarily a helpful one either.

Next, total all the numbers from the women's characteristics and then total the numbers from the men's characteristics. If your totals are higher for women's characteristics than for men's, this means that you value gender-specific qualities that make women "women." You may feel comfortable with traditional femininity and may not see any need to alter this perspective.

If your totals are higher for men's characteristics than women's, you may feel frustrated and limited by your situation and have a strong desire to possess the qualities or characteristics of men to achieve your dreams.

The real key to being a brave woman, however, is not to classify any of the characteristics or qualities on your list as being female or male, but as human qualities that are detached from gender. To be open to the full expression of human characteristics, to feel free to express them and to know that you possess them is to unleash the bravery that drives you to achieve your life's goals, purpose, and meaning.

When you really think about differences, you see a spectrum; you realize that both men and women have all of the characteristics that you've listed. It's a matter of degree. And degree is a matter of what you feel you should express based on your gender and what's expected of you.

Frances: A Brave New Path

One of the "poster girls" interviewed for this book was a young woman named Frances whose attitudes and lifestyle exemplify the characteristics of the brave new you. Frances strikes a healthy balance among intelligence, character, and appearance. She is a scientist, wife, and a proud daughter, who loves clothes, is honest, takes responsibilities for her choices, and thinks critically about herself and her life.

At thirty, Frances not only has her MBA, but a Ph.D. in molecular biology. To make a bold career move, Frances risked taking a job in a city that required she leave her husband and pets during the week. She combines the two degrees in her work at a biotech company just outside of Boston, Massachusetts. Her husband supported Frances while she was earning her degrees, and they worked on their MBA's simultaneously. Her science training allows Frances to make decisions and take risks without allowing her emotions to hold too much sway. "My husband calls me a hard box of rocks. He's the softy. There has to be a huge boulder in my way before I despair or resort to emotional indulgences."

Frances and her husband play to their natural strengths. Their lives are shaped by conscious, well-deliberated choices rather than by following conventional gender roles that would restrict either partner's potential for growth. Frances' mother, who spent many years in a successful, more traditional marriage, not only accepts her daughter's lifestyle choices, but is applying the same principles to her own life.

Become Comfortable with Power

As women enter into all aspects of contemporary life, most tend to have problems with power. Power is the ability to influence and motivate others, and many women are still the ones being influenced or taking orders rather than giving them. Even women in leadership roles for many years feel uncomfortable promoting themselves or feel like imposters or illegitimate if they achieve "too much success."

Shirley Gordon (2001) has spent the greater part of her adult life involved in the field of public policy. Her greatest impact has been to empower other women and advocate for reproductive rights through Planning Advocates of New York State, an organization Shirley founded in 1977. Still, she admits to falling prey to "The Imposter Syndrome," a woman's belief that she's not supposed to be where she is or that "they're going to find out that 'I'm just little Shirley Gordon.'"

Other women at the pinnacle of professional success unconsciously sabotage their powerful image. Kathlyn Hatch, an architectural consultant who travels the world and routinely encounters women in powerful positions, finds it curious to observe that a large number of female CEOs wears three and a half inch heels to meetings. "It's as if they have to mediate their power by accentuating their femininity through these shoes. Women who are comfortable with power and themselves wear comfortable walkers."

Myths and Misconceptions

To think like a brave woman you need to wipe away the myths and misconceptions that prevent you from shooting for the moon or even landing on the stars. Ask yourself the following questions. See how many myths are holding you back or are disempowering you.

Myth No. 1

Do you think that presenting yourself as competent or smart detracts from your femininity and appeal?

There is a myth that presenting yourself as smart or competent is the kiss of death to femininity or attractiveness. In fact, the essence of real appeal and emotional health is the feeling of well-being and confidence that a woman exudes. It's that certain "something" that draws people to her. Part of this appeal is the ability to be a good communicator and to argue with zest, be direct and forthcoming, and enjoy participating in exchange and banter.

But it is also the ability to be aware, to listen and pay attention to others without her own diminishment or loss of presence. This makes a woman even more charismatic and sexy. True, you will always have the detractors who prefer a woman to be "old-fashioned," coy, and alluring without the hint of having any substance, thoughts, or ideas of importance. But as a brave woman this simply isn't appealing.

It's amazing how the majority of women's magazines have "dumbed down" their feature articles and eliminated anything that smacks of "feminism." Most articles are driven by sexual performance or idealized appearances. From articles about "Celebrity Sex Secrets" and "Sixty Ways to Please a Man in Bed" to "How to Lose Ten Pounds in a Week and Feel Healthier and Better about Yourself," women learn not to be satisfied with who they are or how they think. Naturally, they buy into the frustrating and self-defeating obsessions of always looking better and being better. These beliefs run deep and are damaging to your self-concept.

Myth No. 2

Do you believe that women's and men's behavior and emotional lives are worlds (maybe even planets) apart?

Why are there such differences between the way men and women think and feel about themselves, and particularly how they communicate? Is it because men and women come from different planets, as has been suggested? Does biology compel women to communicate more with others and seek professional help quicker for problems than men? Is that why women are considered better team players, more nurturing, and more caring and sensitive to others' needs?

Not necessarily. Women make choices and act in certain ways, not because of their *biology*, but because of their *socialization*: how their families, schools, the media, books, and magazines shaped and molded their thinking and their ideas about women's status in the world.

Power dictates how people communicate with each other in relationships. The person with the most power and authority in a situation or relationship communicates less and is more reserved than the person with less status and authority who communicates more and needs more people to communicate with for support. Reverse the power differential between men and women and you get a role reversal: men communicating more and women less—this is obviously not biology talking. It involves the issue of power and status between men and women, with men in the predominate role, at least for the most part.

For instance, men are not as self-critical as women. Men are less concerned with looks, aging, body weight, and what they say and do. Only because the messages they receive are poles apart from what's communicated to women.

As was explored earlier, to believe in gender-based thinking—that is, it isn't in your "makeup" as a woman to be logical, results-oriented, or business-minded—cuts off your possibilities and choices before you even start. The rug is pulled out from under you, your choices are limited, and you are powerless if you think this way. Your biological destiny does not determine your professional talents and abilities, rather your success is based on what you think you can do and deserve to do.

Myth No. 3

Do you believe that power and status have nothing to do with gender?

A brave woman experiences a sense of *positive entitlement*, the confidence of feeling free to go after her place in the world, and *natural status*, the perception that the world and its opportunities are open to her, just as they have always been to men. She's not a sidekick to someone else's authority and success. Her courage allows her to move against the limiting stereotypes that have imprisoned women.

She will not be pigeonholed as to what she is and can do; she will do what's best for her against the enormous pressure for her to conform.

Your beliefs about these issues, which you will examine in the exercises at the end of this chapter, tell you where you stand with yourself, where you're heading, the choices that you can make and the life that you can live.

Even though there are greater opportunities for women than ever before, women are still limited and limit themselves to low paying service work and the increasingly low paying "helping" professions. Male-dominated professions pay more; female-dominated professions pay less. Status and prestige in male-dominated professions is high, while status and prestige in female professions suffers. That is part of the gender status differential and the brave woman will have none of it.

Myth No. 4

Do you think that women are empathetic and nice, and men are Neanderthals?

Men's versus women's morality is an extremely complex and well-debated issue. Since the early 1980s, when Carol Gilligan (1982) pioneered studies that point out that women's moral development should not be based on male standards, her and her colleagues theories, i.e., that women's values and sense of fairness derive from their gender's orientation toward caring for others, forced other psychologists and scholars studying women's behavior to revise their views. Essentially for Gilligan, women exhibit "an ethic of care." Men's moral development, on the other hand, comes from their gender's sense of justice and drive toward autonomy or independence.

You can probably think of many incidents in your own life where it was a woman and not a man who undermined your career or betrayed you in other ways. It's naïve to think that women are "nice" and can't possibly be as cutthroat, competitive, and ruthless as some men. Women, in fact, feel competition and the threat of loss of status and authority more keenly than men, because it's harder for women to achieve positions of authority and power and even harder for them to hold on to them once they have them.

Gender-based morality is a fiction based on women's socialization to be nice and compliant. It's a theory that has outlived its usefulness. Bravery transcends gender. It is a sterling human quality that evokes admiration even when witnessed over centuries. Think of Antigone, the hero of Sophocles' great play who died for burying her slain brother, an act that defied the rule of law, or Joan of Arc, that other martyr who bravely led her dauphin's troops into battle.

Expect More to Get More

How you feel about yourself, the way you think, fantasize, and idealize reality determines what you expect out of life. Your expectations may come from an idealized view of how you think things should be, and what you've been told. It's hard not to buy into idealized versions of life. They're all around you. After all, sitcom families neatly solve their problems: all is understood and forgiven at the end of the half hour, and there are plenty of laughs throughout the show, so everyone seems witty and upbeat.

Many people accept the images that constantly bombard them; and many believe the *People* magazine celebrity lifestyle is what they want and how it should be. They confuse what their hearts are saying from what others are saying to them. It's hard to hear an inner voice with all the constant clutter and interference.

Many people believe society's perfection myth, which tells you that you must be healthy and happy at all times, you must create storybook holidays for family and friends, take family vacations en masse, never be depressed or angry. You must be able to manage and handle life's vicissitudes with aplomb. Although you are savvy enough and your logic and reason tell you it's fiction, the emotional appeal of the storybook lifestyle is so strong that you may still try to make it real.

When you have very elevated and unrealistic expectations about others, yourself, and the world you face, you set yourself up for unhappiness and disappointment. Being good enough isn't good enough. The gap between what you expect and what really happens can lead to major frustration, disappointments, unhappiness, self-criticism, and disgust for not measuring up to unrealistic ideals.

These *failures in idealism* erode your sense of well-being, your self-worth, and confidence. You believe that the "beautiful people" in this world actually exist and have few blemishes or problems like yours. You think that everyone else is out there having fun, or has the perfect sex life or marriage; others are born with extraordinary qualities that a mere mortal such as you can never possess.

A woman can't be brave and forge ahead with these disabling thoughts as her guide and yardstick. To change, you must separate the genuine article from the false, and stop panning for fool's gold. Revise your expectations; change the ground rules about people and relationships, and you'll marvel at your progress and sense of well-being.

For example, many people, but women especially, expect understanding and empathy for the travails and difficulties they face. They believe that if others provide the support they need, then they'll feel better and, in turn, get better. If they don't receive the necessary support and understanding, they will have a tougher time feeling and doing better for themselves, and have much greater difficulty in improving themselves.

In reality, few people can truly understand or appreciate what you're going through. Actually, lack of empathy is not the problem. The problem is the belief that without empathy and understanding from others you can't change or grow. You can change all on your own. Sure, it nice to have others' support, but holding on to this belief hampers your ability to move on with your life.

Expectations about How You Should Be Treated

Late one Friday afternoon, Mary was walking with a colleague through a large parking lot at her university when she heard loud screams and saw a car parked in the middle of a lane blocking traffic. As they moved closer, the shouting grew louder, and then she and her friend saw a scarlet-faced undergraduate pounding his fists into the hood of his car and shouting ear-splitting obscenities at his hysterical girlfriend.

The young man's rage was so intense and all consuming, he didn't notice the passersby but kept up his tirade, poking his finger in the girl's face to punctuate each four-letter word he uttered. The girl was red-faced and crying, but still returning his verbal volleys with some of her own until he smacked her across the face. He jumped in his car, locked the doors, and started pulling away.

"Please don't leave me, please don't leave me," she screamed, all the while running beside his moving car. "I promise I'll do want you want. Just don't leave me, please. I won't be able to live." This scene of romantic violence flashed in Mary and her friend's minds as a minipreview of this young woman's future domestic life and the probability that at age seventeen or eighteen, she is already suffering from "The Battered Women's Syndrome," a psychological trap in which a woman loses her self-esteem and continues to believe the cycle of abuse will end.

For a while, the young woman put up a good fight, in the only way she knew how, cursing back at her boyfriend and sobbing wildly. Her bravery departed once her boyfriend started pulling away. Somewhere deep inside her, she believed that his verbal and physical violence were preferable to being alone.

The violence in the college parking lot may seem extreme, but, unfortunately, this type of scene repeats itself all over the world every hour of every day.

Women of all ages and educational levels can have low expectations about the way men should treat them. Some women are so grateful and feel so fortunate to have a man in their lives that they will overlook every transgression, every assault. After all, a bad relationship is better than no relationship at all. Many women settle for a quality of life that robs them of their dignity and self-respect. They take on the responsibility and burden of trying to make things work out; they strive to make things better even though their partner is reluctant to share the responsibility or make changes in the relationship.

As a brave woman you will not accept the unacceptable. When you've given it your best shot, when you find that your partner doesn't work with you to improve things, when the finger pointing is always in your direction, then as a brave woman you have a decision to make—one of the most difficult and agonizing of your life. Do you stay or leave? Deep down inside you know the answer. You summon all of your courage to break with the familiar, with the past, with a predictable future that holds little appeal to you. You make your move and break free.

You find that your bravery is now tested more than ever before. When you break the news and see your partner's anger, hurt, and injury, you may become awash with many confusing and contradictory emotions. Your partner's hurt profoundly affects you and you feel guilt. Your partner's injury makes you feel that you're uncaring and insensitive. The anger frightens you, and you feel bad and responsible for the crisis.

You now experience the same overwhelming wave of emotions that have kept you bound and trapped to this relationship in the first place. All the old hurts and patterns are re-enacted. At this point, you must reach into yourself for every ounce of bravery you possess to keep from succumbing to the feelings that have trapped you in this situation in the first place. All your buttons will be pushed to get you to reconsider, to get you to stay put. Don't fall for the promises; don't believe "things will change," because they won't. It will be more of the same and maybe worse for having gone against everything your heart, soul, and mind tell you.

If you go with your bravery, you will be free to heal, change, grow, and find situations and relationships worthy of you.

Inventory Your Relationships

Being treated with dignity and respect is at the heart of mutual and life-enhancing relationships. Make a list of your significant relationships—with family, friends, children, lovers, colleagues, and coworkers. Next to each entry, indicate the nature of the relationship and how it makes you feel.

Which relationships are most satisfactory? Label those with a smiley face. Are there some on the list that need renegotiating? Why? How do they make you feel? If you want to retain the relationship, make a note to create a strategy for talking through some of the things that bother you and set a timetable to follow through.

Are there any relationships on your list that strike you immediately as one-sided, unproductive, and diminish you as an individual? Identity the feelings you associate with these relationships. Think about when and why you became involved with this person. How would you feel if you didn't have this person in your life? Add up the pluses and minuses—what would you lose if you were to end the relationship? What choice best supports your needs?

Expectations about Fairness

Many women believe that if they treat their friends, family, and coworkers with dignity and respect, those same individuals will treat them in kind. This premise, however, is not necessarily true. You desire and expect fairness from others, but more often than not, people relate and communicate differently. Their behavior may be at odds with your expectations of them. When this happens, you're disappointed and disillusioned.

If you present a strong front to people, fearing closeness and being pseudo independent, you may find you expect too little from others. If you feel needy and inadequate in caring for yourself, you may expect too much from others and be crushed when others can't measure up to supplying your emotional and physical needs.

Your belief about fairness extends to events in your life and even to the universe. If you do the right thing, are conscientious, thoughtful, and helpful, you think the universe will protect you from the burdens, trials, and tribulations of life. When this doesn't happen, you feel angry and disappointed and complain about the "unfairness of it all." Complaints turn into cynicism and disillusionment with people and life.

The brave woman knows that not everyone will meet her expectations and not everything will go according to plan. There are always unforeseen surprises that seem to be a godsend, or that are disappointing. As a brave woman you are taking charge of your life, directing your chosen path. You know that there is only so much you can control and influence outside of your own personal sphere; and knowing that, you become powerful and brave. You expect surprises. You expect setbacks and disappointments. Not as a "self-fulfilling prophecy," but in the knowledge that the world is an uncertain place, that tests your resolve, and strengthens you in the face of adversity. Bravery is learning to live with ambiguity and uncertainty.

But as a brave woman, you also know that the world holds for you the promise of something better, and more meaningful. The uncertainty of life gives the brave woman the challenge to overcome. And in overcoming, she gains strength of character, wisdom, and the ability to persevere, making the achievement of her goals that much more sweet and satisfying.

The Influence of Your Expectations

Fairness is often determined by your expectations. Some of you may feel disappointed and let down by other people and events. You give so much and expect others to reciprocate. Others expect very little and are not surprised when they receive little in return. To understand how your expectations shape and color your bravery, you must identify where they fall on the scale from realistic to unrealistic expectations. Check off each statement below that applies to you.

____ When I fall in love, it's with my whole heart and soul.

____ I'm the one who's always calling.

____ I send birthday cards to all my friends and relatives.

____ We always have holidays at our house.

____ I like to pick up the check when I have lunch with my friends.

____ I like to help the hostess clear the table at a dinner party.

____ I bring the cake when someone at work has an anniversary or birthday.

____ I'm always buying little gifts for people.

____ I always give 110 percent of myself to everyone.

If you have checked three or more of these statements, made by people who give a lot and expect a lot in return, you will want to think about and question your expectations and motivations.

Thinking Brave

The brave woman in you expresses flexibility in the "independent/ dependent" continuum. Her beliefs about herself and human nature are balanced. She realizes that there are times when she is dependent on others, when she lacks certain knowledge or resources, or when she needs assistance or guidance with her responsibilities. She is strong and secure enough to know that to lean on someone under these circumstances she is not weak or inadequate to the task, but only human.

She is also independent, in her thoughts and in her actions. There is much that she can do for herself and for others. She is an extension of what is generated within her, her drive for fulfillment, for accomplishment, for success—she is not overly reliant on others for guidance and direction in which she becomes merely an extension of other people's expectations.

The brave woman shines a spotlight on the unexplored landscapes of her being throughout her life's journey. And in this process, she develops superior problem-solving skills, dealing with adversity and with success more effectively than other women do in similar circumstances.

Chapter 4

Face Your Hidden Secrets

Get Real and Power Your Bravery

Just tell the truth. It'll save you every time.

—Oprah Winfrey

All women have secret selves, thoughts, and desires. Secrets about how they feel about themselves and other people. Secrets with girlfriends, sisters, and mothers. Secrets about what they can and cannot do, and about what they really want to do and become.

Some secrets are scary to acknowledge because they threaten some personal, deeply held beliefs. Some secrets are so meaningful that they beckon you to take action, yet you may not feel courageous enough to act on them. Other secrets are based on dreams and wishes that seem unattainable. Maybe you bury these secrets and deny them even to yourself.

These unspoken, unacknowledged secrets gnaw at you. They make you uncomfortable and ill at ease. They whisper from your deep, inner voice, summon you to face your circumstances, your future, and yourself. It's time to be brave, to make a personal commitment, and to create your own life.

Dynamic strategy No. 4 is to know what your secrets are, face them honestly and uncritically, and assess them for their usefulness and practicality. Do they serve the purposes for the brave new you? Even if they seem silly and impractical, remember, many of your secrets are an expression of what you feel is lacking in your life and in you.

Secrets also tell you what you want but are afraid to go after. Secrets provide you with a false sense of comfort, but at the sacrifice of your true passions and bravery. Secrets are precious. They are thoughts and feelings you can never seem to translate into bold action and purpose, or they are thoughts about yourself, other people, or situations about which you are embarrassed. They surface from the shadow or dark side of your nature.

The Power of Secrets

Your bravery puts you face-to-face with your hidden secrets. Once you see them they lose their power over you. Then your "public self," the outer shell that you have constructed for others, and the inner shell of secrets you've adopted for yourself disappear. You will feel relieved, energetic, hopeful, and determined, and you'll revel in the freedom that comes from liberating your heart and mind to the truth of your whole being. As you live as your authentic self, you become powerful, you become brave.

Being more authentic and less false is difficult to accomplish. Much of your energy is spent "creating" an illusion of yourself, a self-image, that mirrors back what you crave from the world—fame, power, celebrity, friendship, and even security. The drives to "have it all" and to appear to "have it all together" are all consuming and leave little time for self-reflection and the personal growth required to become aware of your authentic self. The paradox is that when you give up inventing an artificial self that masks your real one, you allow yourself to connect with your natural humanity. Only then do you begin to live authentically and with bravery.

Brilliant Disguises

Is that you, baby, or just a brilliant disguise?

—Bruce Springsteen

In this age of "virtuality" and computer-generated aliases, you have even more ways to disguise and distance yourself from what psychologists call your *authentic self.* Your authentic self is your true self, you *au natural,* unadorned, straightforward, direct, unembellished—the kind of woman others have a high regard for and point to as "what you see is what you get."

Kit: Living in Virtual Reality

Kit, a New York State University student, embodies a woman who literally lost touch with her real identity. She revealed her secret life during a candid discussion in class about the Internet and its impact on personality. Kit confessed that for three semesters she had been spending in excess of eight hours per day online. She had stopped seeing friends outside of class, and her long-distance relationship with her boyfriend was suffering, because he could never get through on the line. Sitting in front of the computer, her eyes glued to the monitor, she barely studied and just got by in her classes, ate her meals at her computer desk, and hardly talked with her roommates.

Kit was living her life in chat-rooms. "It's much more exciting than my real life," she told her classmates. E-mail, cyber-chatting with strangers enabled her to be anyone she wanted to pretend to be. Online she could be a man and express her power, she could be intimate, even though she was timid in her everyday dealings with others. "I was daring, Professor, and you know how afraid I am to speak up in class."

Addictions, such as Kit spending long hours on the Internet, create a disconnect with the pulse of inner being from which your bravery springs. In this instance, her compulsive behavior completely submerged much of her personality and identity. She was rapidly losing touch with who she really was, and role-playing through her Internet addiction subsumed her inner dialogue and self-reflection.

Kit was everything but who she truly is. She was fast becoming a virtual reality. She didn't realize that being a virtual creation, something other than herself, was a form of self-rejection that would lead to dissatisfaction, a lack of self-fulfillment, and an empty life. Her need to escape from herself was reflected in the quality of her relationships with others. Other people failed to respect her or turned away—not because they didn't like or admire her, but because she had lost self-respect.

Kit is an extreme but common example of how cyber-age technologies, by their very nature, tend to facilitate and accentuate the gap between a real self and a virtual one, a fictitious creation that some may accept as real, but, in fact, is not. The computer becomes an intermediary with the world. Even before the technological revolution, many people presented virtual selves to the world to fulfill others' expectations, even though authenticity was lost in the process.

To varying degrees, almost everyone creates public selves that mask true intentions and disguise true identities. The game of "let's pretend," however, deprives you of the ability to be brave and test your mettle in the real world.

The Dark Side of the Light Chasers author and motivator Debbie Ford (1999) puts it this way: "People who 'know it all' are usually covering up feelings of stupidity, while those who act arrogantly have yet to reveal their insecurity. The cool people are hiding the geek within, and the smiling face, an angry one. We have to look beyond our social masks to discover our authentic selves. We are masters of disguise, fooling others but fooling ourselves" as well (57).

Women and Their Ancient Secrets

Women and secrets have been an item since the Garden of Eden. In folklore and myth, women carry the forbidden fruit that changes the destiny of peoples' lives and how they see themselves and the world around them.

In Greek mythology, Pandora, the first woman made by the gods, unlocks a box of secrets she wasn't supposed to open and all the worlds' sins or blessings escape. Eve couldn't resist a taste of the forbidden either, so she bit into the apple to taste the secrets of the knowledge of good and evil and a life of self-awareness.

Depending on how you interpret these bold women's acts, Pandora and Eve are either passionate questers in search of new knowledge and their human possibilities or examples of women who can't keep a secret, no matter what.

It is woman in these stories who makes a man aware of his nature. She provides him with choices and self-awareness, gives him an understanding of the reality of the human condition. She removes his mask of innocence and initiates him into the realities of good and evil. And for this, women have been condemned. Since then, women have been reluctant to reveal the true nature about themselves and others for fear of retribution. A little honesty can be a dangerous thing.

The babushka doll is another woman with a secret. Pull her apart and there's another one of her concealed inside. Pull this next one apart and there is another secret doll hiding inside her, and so on. You pick her up and take pleasure in opening all of her compartments until all the little secret dolls are revealed. Peeling off the layers of the false selves and coming upon the hidden parts and secrets is a more difficult and complex process. These layers are self-imposed and self-protective.

The "I Am Perfect" Secret

Are you a driven overachiever who presents the perfect picture of yourself as super competent to the world?

In a culture that worships glitz, glamour, and image, it's the surface of things that seems to count. All too easily, people think the road maps of consumerist culture are the source of the inner quest for honesty, authenticity, and aliveness. It is falsely believed that acquiring things or becoming wired to the world on cell phones or the information superhighway is a passport to status, happiness, popularity, and personal satisfaction.

When satisfaction doesn't occur, the dead end of attaining purely material needs and desires is revealed. You feel more lost and empty than ever. Cynicism and disillusionment increase because you realize that the only road maps handed to you (and the ones that you thought you could accept) don't bring you to the place you want to be. You remain disillusioned and cynical, even though the picture you present to the world is perfect.

Deana: Perfect to Everyone but Herself

Deana grew up in a lower middle class family in western Massachusetts. The only girl among four boys and the middle child, she was the smartest in her high school classes and at the state university where she majored in communications. Perhaps from competing with four brothers or because of her economic circumstances and putting herself through school, Deana drove herself to be the best. Anything less than that was unacceptable. She put enormous pressure on herself and felt the need to constantly prove herself in ways that didn't require wearing the latest fashion or driving a "hot" car.

She was the most competent communications officer in the governor's office by age thirty-three, and a year later, she was on the fast track in Washington, D.C., as the advance person for a state senator. She wore designer suits and carried designer handbags. She knew where to get her hair done when in New York, whom to call for stock tips in L.A., where to buy the best truffles in the Hamptons, the latest exercise guru, the most intriguing foreign films. She had a live-in relationship with the perfect partner: he was an assistant producer at CNN, and his family had a beach house on Nantucket Island where they would spend two weeks in the summer. Her life was a whirlwind of successful status seeking.

For three years Deana felt on top of the world and in total control of her life. The only downside was that her friends were starting to shy away from her. She noticed that despite all her success, she was becoming more judgmental and intolerant of others.

Her need to be in the know or perfect wasn't the expression of herself but the manifestation of her deepest, darkest fear that she really wasn't up to snuff. Instead of enjoying a life filled with creative expressions, fulfillment, peace of mind, and bravery, she lived with doubt, anxiety, and the terror of being found out that she was really a big nothing, a fraud with little to offer.

Like many women, viewed her life in absolutes: Either she was a total success in every way or she was a disastrous failure beyond redemption. The power of the inner forces that were driving Deana was in direct proportion to her inability to face the truth about herself. Because she was too busy being "perfect," she was unable to be authentic.

Losing Yourself by Seeking Perfection

The drive to be perfect or supercompetent wrests control from your life and makes you feel impotent and powerless to adjudicate your own decisions about who you want to be and what you want for yourself. Your bravery evaporates under the sway of any addiction, or compulsion, that rules your life.

You might latch on to addictions and compulsions to regain control of yourself, but then find that your addictions or compulsions control you instead. You just "do" things—not from your convictions, values, and beliefs, but because it's what's expected of you, it's not what you expect from yourself. You "morph" yourself into the expectations that others have of you. You confuse *imposed* expectations with the messages coming from within yourself that tell you who you really are, what you really want to accomplish, and who you really want to be.

With time, perfectionism causes you to lose your critical faculty. Increasingly, you fail to think things through or question what you do. You become alienated from yourself, disconnected and empty, your bravery languishes, your secrets pile up and, like Deana, you live a lie, always fearing that you'll be found out.

How Bravery Affects Perfectionism

Taking risks of all sizes and kinds is the antidote to perfectionistic tendencies. The more risks you take, the better you will be able to cope with all kinds of eventualities as they come. Using bravery to risk and cope will increase your self-confidence and self-esteem. You will become more flexible and philosophical and come to realize that your sense of self and sense of success are not tied to *situational failures*, which are experiments in learning, not an expression of who you are.

The "I Have So Much to Do I Can't Think Straight" Secret

Be honest, do you use busyness as your escape from your thoughts and from yourself? Are you so busy being busy that the meaning, value, and the rewards of relationships get lost and find themselves on the proverbial backburner?

The brave woman knows that her pursuit of authenticity, truth, and reality (what she's really about, what she feels, and what she knows) is a very private, inner journey of self-discovery: the road trip she takes alone. This journey requires self-trust and honesty, tuning in, with sensitivity, to the changing landscape of your being, getting in touch with your voice—not the superimposed voice of others or society.

Your inner bravery cannot drive your life if you studiously continue to run away from yourself. Turning off the noise, listening to your inner signals, and discarding the masks of pretense and disguise allow your real self to emerge. You then speak your mind, direct your life, and see opportunities where previously none existed. Many women find that they try to avoid much of their stress and discomfort by filling every minute with activity, every silence with a sound.

Lisa: Losing Herself in Busyness

Lisa is a woman who objectively seems to have it all: a splendid apartment, a country home, fabulous clothes, world travel, an attentive circle of friends, a professional husband, and a grand lifestyle in the lush California wine country above San Francisco. Still, in the midst of her charity work, spending time with her children and grandchildren, and keeping herself in top shape after working for many years as the director of a successful nonprofit organization, Lisa confesses she has lost touch with herself and is very anxious.

"I'm busier than I was when I was working full-time," she says, "but I've gone into therapy, because I'm having trouble being alone. I can't stand silence. In the car, I'm listening to books on tape. I'm having gatherings at home all week, at all hours. I run myself ragged doing mindless errands. I see every play that opens in San Francisco, and then rush up to Sonoma for a tasting, then down to L.A. to see the grandkids. I can't stop and let myself think. My husband, Don, is worried, too, because I can't eat at my own parties or at anybody else's house. I do enjoy preparing and setting up the food for others, but I've lost so much weight, I'm down to a size two."

Like Lisa, many women convince themselves they are leading fulfilling, exemplary lives. When questioned over a period of time, however, they reveal doubts and misgivings about their life choices and significant relationships. After three hours of intense conversation, Lisa broke down and confessed that her marriage had been over for many years. She had only stayed with her husband to maintain her elegant lifestyle and was afraid that at her age, she wouldn't be able to support herself on her own.

How Bravery Affects Time and Authenticity

In twenty-first century culture, hectic schedules, duties, and endless responsibilities crowd out reflection and quiet time in women's lives. They honestly believe that they can and must do it all. On top of which, they believe they should be svelte and glamorous for their partner, if he's going to have any continued interest in them. They're always on diets, trying to create that elusive, yet perfect figure often pictured in magazines and on television. Frustrations mount as women learn firsthand that they can't have superbodies, be supermoms, superwives, and supersuccessful people in everything they do.

- To be brave is to go against popular trends of what you need and how you should look, think, and act as a woman.

- To be brave is to face realistic limitations and to expand on your possibilities You know there is more to life than stepping on a treadmill for most of your day.

- Being brave is to take charge of things and to know when to let go, letting others pick up the slack. To know that you can't please everyone and that's okay—without feeling guilty, or experiencing deep remorse for letting people down, or feeling bad about yourself because you're not a "super" person. You are smart and talented, you know what you're doing most of the time, though not all of the time.

Your busyness gives structure to your life, it gives you a reason for being, it makes you feel important, like the false "status" of talking on a cell phone. This is your excuse and what you must believe to continue to go on in this exhausting unfulfilling way. The busy person on the go is admired. The person who retreats in quiet reflection, who stops and gets off the world, is not.

To be overbusy is to avoid thinking about yourself, being alone, and taking risks. The more you avoid, the less courage you develop and the less confidence you have in your own resourcefulness. You become brave by taking risks—they can be baby steps at first. Your goal is to buoy your bravery: speak your mind, do something creative, relate to someone you admire in a new way, find a new job.

As a brave woman, your worries become real concerns about life, the human condition, and the betterment of humankind. You stop wasting time and energy trying to get love in all the wrong places, but you experience true love in genuine and mature relationships. Admiration, security, power, and peace of mind are already within you. The brave new you stops worrying about what other people think, so you have time to empower yourself and to make the right choices for your life and the quality of your future.

The "I Am Ultra Generous (to a Fault)" Secret

You always give 110 percent of yourself to everyone, and get very little in return. Generosity, giving to others, is an admirable trait. Most women like to think of themselves as generous, and they want others to think of them as giving. Yet compulsive, unregulated, indiscriminate giving, that is giving all the time to any and all, to the deserving and undeserving alike, can result in false giving.

Many women hide this secret from themselves. It is difficult to discover and even to discuss, not only because being overly generous seems like a good quality, but also because it defines who many women are.

Yet like being perfect or being busy, ultragiving is a disguise and hides your true intentions. It can mask the desires to control a situation, to have power over someone, or to thwart others' growth and sense of autonomy. This kind of ultragiving to children is overwatering and flooding the roots without giving them the wings to fly on their own.

Marcia: Keeping Track of Generosity

Marcia is known as the best cook, the best mother, and the best friend anyone could imagine. She wouldn't think of having friends over for a pick-me-up or take-out meal. On her table, the breads are homemade, the fish freshly caught, the silverware polished to perfection. Her home is a stage set where guests sit on pedestals. They never clear away the dishes and are encouraged to relax and enjoy themselves. Her husband and children also feel like guests in their home. All she wants them to do is to "be their charming selves" and entertain friends with their wit and brilliance.

When her friends are down and out or ill, Marcia is there with her famous chicken soup. She calls to cheer them up and even cooks dinners for their families. Her children are devoted to her. She calls them four or five times a day, even now when they're out on their own, and she pays many of their bills, treats them to vacations, a new computer, any extra that provides them pleasure and ease. Her love for her children is unconditional. But is it?

Marcia's secret is that she expects others to reciprocate in kind or to treat her like a queen because they owe so much to her. She never comes out and says anything, but she sulks in silence or plays Joan of Arc. Like the Energizer bunny, she keeps giving and giving, building up a case and keeping a tally against those who slight her or don't pay her back.

Marcia lives for and through others. She has set up a network of indebted family and friends who have no idea what she's really thinking and take advantage of her generosity. Marcia has not yet taken her own risks or explored her bravery.

How Bravery Affects Generosity

Being habitually overgenerous goes hand in hand with fears of rejection and abandonment, or being criticized if you don't please others. You cannot be authentic and honest if you base your behavior on fear. Use bravery to counteract your fear impulses.

The brave woman is measured. She gives from a place of genuine caring rather than of neediness or because she "should." Your generosity will come from a place of genuine thoughtfulness, when you stop overgiving. You won't give to gain favors or acceptance. You won't have the need to please people or appear needy. Another bonus? You will eliminate exploitative people in your life. People-pleasers are magnets for exploiters.

The Real Secret to Bravery: Self-Acceptance

The brave woman knows the greatest liberating secret that continues to ignite and sustain her bravery is self-acceptance. Self-acceptance doesn't mean approval, or right or wrong behavior or thinking. It means facing yourself and embracing all the facets of your humanity, the acceptable with the unacceptable. This is a brave act, but a very important one, if we are going to take our secrets public, recognize and acknowledge them.

You don't have to let everything "hang out," for there is discretion regarding the expression of your bravery, honesty, and integrity. As a brave woman, you know when to take a stand, and when not to waste your time in lost causes. You discover that you understand the world only when you understand yourself. Outer revelation comes through inner knowing.

By increasing self-acceptance, you unleash the power of your bravery in ways that you can't even begin to imagine. You become forceful, yet considerate, you speak your mind about your needs, wishes, dreams, and your future without holding others responsible for your well-being and life fulfillment. You can tell others what you like and don't like. You speak in a powerful yet nonthreatening manner because your voice comes from your core self and not from a place of putting someone down, or exacting revenge.

To be authentic is to be brave; to be brave is to be powerful; to be powerful is to have choices; to have choices is the freedom of fulfillment and true and lasting purpose in life.

What you learn about how you should be may actively oppose who you are and affect your ability to accept what you are. You must see yourself for who you are, you must accept yourself. You then become brave.

If you continue to experience secrets to the extent that you - censor your dreams and inner longings, your wishes and fantasies, then you may mold yourself exclusively to the expectations of others and fail to recognize the expectations that you have of yourself. You'll become depressed, angry, anxious, vindictive, critical, and judgmental.

Your bravery expands your consciousness by removing the blindfold that covered your eyes. Suddenly, you can see things that were always in front of you but you couldn't see before. It's not that your environment provides you with more choices, but that you have changed and *allowed* yourself to see those choices and opportunities to which you were previously not open. Your emerging bravery and enhanced self-acceptance will allow you to express who you really are, and to say and do what you really want.

Total Honesty as a Policy

Your growth, the person you want to be and become, the life you want to lead, the consistent expression of your bravery, all require total honesty with yourself, even if it hurts—and being honest with yourself commonly does. Being honest with yourself means lowering enough of your defenses to see yourself and situations more clearly, more realistically. *Defenses* are any entrenched pattern of behavior or thought that you express spontaneously to protect your perception of yourself and the world. Defenses guard you from real or imagined pain either in the past or in the present.

Some defenses are no longer useful, in fact, they hurt your chances for growth and success, for better relationships, and a better life. They are emotionally draining and suck the life force out of your bravery, the engine that drives against resistances that slow you down and stop you in your tracks.

Writing Your Self

Keep a daily journal of your thoughts, feelings, the day's events, your reactions to things, memories, etc. Allow your writing to flow into your journal without hesitation, without censorship. Remember the journal is private and only for you. By writing in your journal daily, the writing in itself will reveal long-buried thoughts, feelings, and wishes. A journal helps you to create sense out of a jumble of thoughts and feelings you may have. Writing at least three or four pages a day will serve as a conduit into your deepest dreams, desires, and thoughts about your life.

Telling Your Secrets

Besides writing in your journal, which will put you in touch with the secret life that goes on inside of you, spelling out your secrets will allow you to truth-tell, which means unpacking your secrets and exposing the raw truth of what you tell yourself and what underlies your dealings with others.

Truth-telling comes about after you face the lies you tell yourself and reveal the hidden beliefs about yourself and others that separate you from the authentic woman you can become. Check off each of the common "lies" or hidden beliefs listed below that you tell yourself and other people.

Lies/Hidden Beliefs You Tell Yourself

____ I'm unlovable.

_____ I'm not good enough.

_____ I'm a failure.

_____ I'm unattractive.

_____ I'm stupid.

_____ I can't.

_____ I'm too old to change my life or my circumstances.

_____ The time is not right.

_____ I'm afraid (to be) (to have) (to create) _____ .

_____ I'm a coward at heart, being brave is not in my nature.

_____ I can't take risks or do things differently because I have too many responsibilities.

_____ I'm too scared to take risks.

_____ If I feel bad that means I've done something wrong.

_____ I'm too busy doing for others to do anything for myself.

_____ I will always be alone.

_____ I will never be happy.

Lies/Hidden Beliefs You Tell Other People

_____ That didn't bother me, I'm above his/her manipulations.

_____ Don't worry about me, I'm doing just fine.

_____ I don't care what other people think.

_____ I'm different, other people can't touch me.

_____ I said that to you because I'm only trying to help you.

_____ I can't act differently because that's the way I *feel.*

_____ You never appreciate me no matter what I do for you.

_____ You should know how I feel, I shouldn't have to tell you.

_____ I can't live without you no matter what you do to me.

_____ You should always be there for me when I need you.

_____ I can never trust you.

_____ If you were really thoughtful and considerate of me I wouldn't need to ask you for your help.

_____ If you really cared and loved me you wouldn't have any quarrels with me.

_____ I'm upset with you, which means you're deliberately trying to hurt my feelings.

_____ You men (women) are all alike.

If you checked off five or more items in each part, you definitely need to work on being more honest with yourself, with other people, and about your situation. If you checked off more than eight items in each list, you might want to consider talking with a reputable counselor who can help you make a realistic assessment of yourself and work with you to become more in touch with your real feelings and emotions.

How Beliefs Shape Your Bravery

Hidden secrets are the beliefs you have about situations that, and people who, predominantly affect your life. Your ability to be brave is shaped by what you believe about yourself, about others, about circumstances, and about the world and human nature in general. As you learned from the exercise above, you can only go as far as your beliefs allow you to go and no .

Some woman are brave "overachievers" because of what they believe about themselves and about their life goals. Most women, underachieve. They have beliefs that limit their abilities and possibilities. They don't have the courage to succeed because of their limiting beliefs, beliefs that they may not think about consciously, but nevertheless rule their life and destiny.

Remember that beliefs are what you *think* reality is about. Beliefs, however, create your reality, not the other way around. Because of this phenomenon, changing your beliefs changes the reality of who you are, what you are capable of doing, how you can conduct your life, and how you can be brave in far greater ways than you may believe possible.

The following questions will help you to expose some of your previously unexamined beliefs. In your journal, answer the following questions honestly.

- Do you have the secret thought that life is passing you by and that you have little to show for it? Write about it.

- Do you belief that life is a series of "lucky breaks" that you haven't been able to cash in on? Why do you think this is true for you?

- Do you think that there may be alternate explanations for what has happened in your life? What do you think these alternate explanations might be?

Look back at your responses to this series of questions. Have you taken responsibility? If you harbor the secret that life is passing you by and you have little to show for it, you may be an observer and not a participant in shaping your destiny. If you think that life is a series of lucky breaks, think again. Lucky breaks only come when all the hard work is done. Finally, you are responsible for what happens in your life. No one else. No excuses. The brave woman takes responsibility for herself and her life, she pilots the ship and directs her course.

It is an empowering and brave way to recognize that you control your destiny and make life choices, up to a point. However, everyone starts on an unequal playing field. Some women begin with fewer opportunities and greater obstacles because of where and to whom they were born. Temperaments and personalities also help or hinder various stages of life. These explanations are not excuses, but the awareness of your situations may help you to take responsibility for your life and to do so despite your circumstances.

Secrets about People

The people you surround yourself with reveal volumes about yourself. To be the brave new you is to know and accept your thoughts and feelings about other people. Some secrets you harbor about people may be highly unflattering. In this instance, it's wise to keep these beliefs and thoughts to yourself.

Don't judge yourself too harshly for having these feelings. And don't accept that you are wrong or "sick" for having them. You may not always like what you feel about circumstances or people, but most everyone harbors harsh opinions of others from time to time. You have hidden secrets to the extent that you feel prohibited from expressing them.

Exposure through Writing

Write down some secret feelings you have about people in your past or present life. Record anything—situations or experiences that are positive, negative, charged, or supercharged. Notice the emotions that well up as you write. Are the feelings intense? Do they seem to have a life of their own? Does any one person dominate your thoughts?

You can handle your feelings, no matter what they are, without beating up on yourself. Feel, fantasize, and write down everything. You never have to act out any destructive feelings about which you write. Simply know that by being human you will have positive and negative feelings throughout your life. It's important that you simply accept this truth without self-criticism or self-condemnation.

Accepting this knowledge is empowering because you don't hide or run away from what you feel. As a result, you don't accumulate a residue of anger, anxiety, frustration, or depression. You free up that energy to empower your dreams, wishes, circumstances, and your talents to achieve your true purposes in life. As you face your true purpose, which is your greatest secret, you are becoming the brave women that you secretly always knew you were but might have been afraid to acknowledge.

Your Secret Dreams

Are you afraid to dream big because you fear being disappointed? Some people have been hurt and disappointed so many times that they vow never again to have high hopes or expectations. Many are too afraid that what they yearn for will not come about and, therefore, they cease to dream. Instead, they plan and settle for the ordinary and mundane, submerging their bravery because their passion for something better is gone.

Penning Your Disappointments into Dreams

Writing about disappointment can help you to recall and possibly to enact your bravest hopes and passions. In your journal, explore the following questions. Be sure to write freely, not judging or censoring your answers.

- What does disappointment mean to you?

- What are some of the significant disappointments of your past?

- What do you *feel* as thoughts about disappointment come to your mind?

- Do you feel that you're carrying the impact of past disappointments into your present circumstances?

- How have your disappointments affected your dreams, your successes, and the bravery needed to make your life a masterpiece of fulfillment?

Bravery is a passion that will transport you beyond the ordinary and into the realm where the extraordinary can happen. For your bravery to take hold and charge your life, you must think and dream expansively and globally. Continuous improvement, growth, and satisfaction, and contribution to a better world requires perseverance, vision, and honesty.

Chapter 5

Shoot Down Your Major Fears

Be Brave in Every Part of Your Life

Usually we think that brave people have no fear.
The truth is they are intimate with fear.

—Pema Chödron

A comedy writer from White Plains, New York, says she lives her life according to a quote she once heard as a young girl: "Never grow a wishbone, daughter, where your backbone ought to be." The brave woman has backbone. She asserts her bravery in the face of fear and develops the inner security to know when to give in to a situation and when to take healthy control of it. Bravery never surrenders to the fear that situations fall apart when a woman speaks her mind and stands up for herself.

Dynamic strategy No. 5 is learning that fear and change are necessities for—not enemies of—the brave woman. Pushing through your fears and acting bravely in every area of your life builds self-confidence and increases your sense of influence regarding your life.

The brave woman is "intimate with fear." It's a signal that she's moving into unfamiliar and uncharted territory. By entering into her "discomfort zone," the brave woman stays with her fear, she lives and breathes it, becoming intimately acquainted with it being inside her as she allows the fear-based sensation to settle in her body.

Learning to accept fear is achieved by rewiring your feelings and associations around it. Each time you experience fear, try to associate its sensations—stomach butterflies, a knot in your throat, moist palms, a quickening pulse—with excitement and exhilaration rather than trepidation. Think of it this way: You're out on a limb, ready to meet the challenge, and it's your moment to break through to a new adventure.

Become Intimate with Fear

The brave woman knows that fear is unavoidable, inescapable really, and so she partners with it, knowing that fear is created by new challenges and opportunities. Pushing through fear takes her to new levels of bravery and fearlessness. What the brave woman once feared, she no longer does. Instead, she takes action despite the fear. By repeating her actions, she becomes comfortable in what previously was the "fear zone."

What Exactly Is Fear?

The majority of fears are beliefs that you *think* are true. In most cases, fears are created based on some irrational belief or real-life exposure to danger. Typically, fears create some type of paralysis, which prohibits you from changing your life and/or your circumstances.

Fear causes you to invent an inner dialogue of false beliefs about yourself. These beliefs are not as deeply rooted or as ingrained as when they are part of your core personality and the beliefs you retain from childhood. Nevertheless, they are compelling and induce you to limit your choices or to feel as if you have no choice.

As a brave woman you know that fear is a *feeling*, not an event. Knowing this, you push through your fears to achieve your ambitions. Your bravery is based on feeling your fear and taking action *in spite* of it.

Identify and Name Your Fears

To name your fears is to begin to rein them in and have influence over them, making them smaller and more manageable. It is emotionally difficult to experience fear without understanding from where it's really coming. When you can't identify the origin of your fear, it can become overwhelming and paralyzing, reducing you to a footnote in your own life history. Identifying your fears is the prelude for allowing the brave new you to emerge.

Break Open Your Fears: An Exercise

The next babushka doll represents your fears and trepidations. Break it open and look at the anxieties that cause you to panic or to become alarmed. On a piece of paper or in your journal, create a "Top Ten List" of your major fears. Be brave in your assessment. Fears speak directly to your level of self-confidence and self-esteem, and calibrate how assertive you are.

What is your number one fear? Are you, like a majority of people, terrified to speak in public? (Fear of public speaking is on the top of many people's list, even ahead of death.) Are you afraid to ask your mate to share the household chores with you? Does your stomach tie up in knots at the thought of asking your boss for a raise? Are you afraid to say "no" to people because you fear hurting their feelings or letting them down? Do you fear not meeting other people's needs when they expect you to?

What about your private fears and your secrets? Are you afraid to be alone? Do you fear making a mistake, saying the wrong thing, or appearing "dumb"? Are you afraid to succeed and get ahead of the pack, because you fear making people jealous and angry with you? Do you think your success will cause you to lose your friends? Do you believe that it's "lonely at the top"? You may have convinced yourself that you don't have what it takes, you're not smart enough, talented enough, you don't know the right people, etc.

The "fear of success" syndrome, formerly known as "The Horner Effect" (Horner 1972), has become part of popular discourse, and has been well documented and studied since the early seventies. Although it fortunately is less potent as a force among women currently in their twenties and thirties, the syndrome refers to women subconsciously underachieving or being afraid to compete for top jobs and positions because they fear the loss of friendships and intimacy.

Face Your Fears

To face your fears you not only need to know what your fears are, but you must also identify which of them are irrational, and which are understandable in certain circumstances. You need to consider if your anxiety represents a real danger or merely something you have blown out of proportion to mask another under-lying fear. Once identified, you must begin to bravely face your fears, either alone, or with the help of a professional or personal sup-port person.

Linda: A Brave New Path

Linda is so afraid of snakes, she can't look at pictures of them, not even in a children's book. She won't go to zoos. When she's at the movies or watching television, she makes sure not to watch National Geographic specials or to view films that take place in Africa or jungle settings. Whether Linda is in nature, in the city, or safely in her living room watching television, the idea and reality of snakes frighten her. Once, while crossing a bridge, Linda brushed shoulders with a man who had an enormous boa draped around his neck and shoulders. Knowing her fear, her companions were shocked and amazed that Linda hadn't flinched or reacted in any way to that close encounter with her terror. Once across the bridge, they asked her, "Did you see that snake?" "What snake?" she replied. Linda hadn't seen the snake, she hadn't even seen the man. She had been literally "blinded by her fear" and denied the reality of it.

When she was two and sleeping in her crib, Linda had been ter-rified when she heard screams coming from her parents' bedroom. After several minutes, her mother appeared and found a garter snake curled around the crib legs. It was a very hot summer day, and the snake had crept into the house to find shade. Her mother, who was also deathly afraid of snakes, screamed when she discovered the reptile. Interestingly, the first screams had nothing to do with the snake, but with her parents' postlovemaking fight. This fear-based double whammy (the snake and her parents' fighting), coupled with Linda's imagination, created a full-blown reptile phobia that she car-ried with her all her life.

Linda's fear of snakes was irrational and persisted, until she intimately and directly faced her fear. With the help of a professional therapist, Linda overcame her fear by engaging with a technique called exposure therapy. First she began to face her fears at a com-fortable distance, looking at pictures, reading stories about them, and viewing nature shows on television. Next, she and her therapist began to interact with real snakes: first they were in cages across the room, then in cages sitting on top of the desk, and, eventually, Linda was capable of remaining unafraid even when a harmless snake would be uncaged on the floor nearby.

When you are willing to face your fears directly, a strange thing happens: the fear loses its intensity and disappears. You are brave enough to look at and directly interact with your fear. As you draw closer, each courageous step toward your fear lessens the fear's grip over you and your life. As a brave woman, you have learned that to face your fears is to conquer them.

Extreme Behaviors Limit Bravery

Any extreme behavior or intense emotion isn't usually what it super-ficially appears to be. As all-or-nothing solutions, emotional extremes are inauthentic and compulsive attempts at resolving issues and problems. They are not genuine. Interestingly extreme tendencies most often magnify true concerns, which commonly are the mirror reflections of original issues.

Complete surrender, for example, is the flip side of complete control. Although one emotion may feel better to you than the other, feeling or enacting one extreme (e.g., control) means you're still at war with the opposite tendency (e.g., surrender). Both surrender and control are performances or pretenses; they are examples of the games you might play with yourself to ward off fear. You tell yourself, if I can surrender so completely, then how can I be so controlling? Or if I'm in control, then how can I possibly give in?

Extreme thinking or acting doesn't occur when you acknowledge and deal with the feelings and behaviors you label as "unacceptable." Instead, you experience balance, the easy flow of give-and-take, a suppleness that allows you to be appropriate in diverse situations.

Reversals of Feelings

Psychologists call extreme, black-and-white behavior a *reaction formation*, which means that you act the opposite of how you really feel to protect yourself from something that you fear in yourself and that you haven't resolved or accepted. For instance, you take up high-risk ventures—bungee jumping, skydiving, or mountain climbing—because deep down inside you *fear* being afraid of heights.

Or you find yourself always trying to please people and cater to their needs—you're always available to them at your expense. You don't act this way because you're nice, you actually fear that you may have controlling, selfish, uncaring, and even hateful impulses toward these same individuals. So you cloak your real, unacceptable feelings under the guise of goodness. You may become extremely moralistic and judgmental, even condemn others for their "evil ways," because you're the one afraid of losing control and expressing your own pleasure-seeking urges.

Moving toward Balance and Interdependence

Extreme behavior is always suspicious because you're not really responding to other people or to particular situations, but to the wishes and fantasies that you deny and repress in yourself. You become free, genuine, and authentic if you don't fear but rather accept your feelings—those that are pleasant as well as those that are unsettling. It doesn't mean that you have to act on your feeling, but it does mean acknowledging and accepting them. You express the courage of your choices, always varying and fluid with your changing circumstances and never rigid in your thoughts and behavior.

The brave woman is consistent and asserts her power and autonomy in every part of her life. Her relationships are authentic, real, and alive. She doesn't need to brag about herself, compete with others, or control them. Her "impression management," a conscious attempt to present a false self to the world, is minimal or nonexistent. She has nothing to prove and no one to impress.

The brave new you is straightforward, yet tactful. You relate to people because you like them and want to share your experiences and your feelings with them. You are not with people because you can get something out of them or because they make good "trophy friends." The hallmark of your relationships is "interdependency." Being interdependent with someone in your close relationships means you can be dependent on others when necessary and independent at other times. You expect others to be in relationship that way with you.

Imagine a Time You Were Fearless: An Exercise

The following exercise will help you identify what it feels like to operate without fear, to learn to be yourself, and to choose friends and companions who support your authenticity.

First close your eyes and remember a time when you felt most at ease and "like yourself": you felt secure, safe with another person, or even in a challenging situation. You were living in the moment without pretense or fear. What did that feel like? How long did it last? Can you duplicate those feelings at this moment?

Now think of another time when you were pretending to be someone you're not. What or whom did you pretend to be? Where were you? How did those around you react?

Next, imagine someone you know who seems fearful or timid. What's that person's impact? How does he or she come across? Think of someone you know who is always "her" or "him" self around you, someone who isn't afraid to be who he/she is. What adjectives would you use to describe him or her?

Finally, create a picture in your mind of yourself in a fear-inducing situation.

Where are you? What are you feeling? Mentally stay in that situation using the above character traits of others to help you cut through and triumph over your fear.

Remember if you continually feel the need to prove yourself over and over again or if you always try to take charge of any and all situations without taking specific circumstances into account, then you are operating from a place of weakness and inadequacy. In essence, you are trying to make sure that the future turns out exactly as you want it, with no surprises, and no disappointments. It's an impossible feat that depletes your resources and limits your life direction.

Fulfilling Your Dreams through Perceived Chaos

Fear is endemic in all people. No one is ever completely free from fears. Both men and women fear failure, criticism, disapproval, or making significant changes in their lives. Most people fear learning unpleasant information about others or themselves. To maintain self-esteem, they cling to what makes them feel secure, what they believe they know. The irony is that when people let go of their security blankets for just one instant and face chaos and uncertainty, they begin to get hold of their dreams.

The safety net of security is not what it seems to be. Security serves the purpose of giving a feeling of safety and allowing certainty in our lives; it creates a certain amount of stability and limits anarchy. You need predictability up to a point for your emotional stability. Problems occur, however, when clinging to "security" begins to hinder and stifle you. The fear of losing your security will always limit you and submerge your bravery, especially when you are afraid to let go and move on to new experiences and challenges.

The brave new you will come to reverence change instead of routine. You will welcome fear and disorder, understanding that security is an illusion.

Shifting Responsibilities of a Multi-Person

As a contemporary woman, your responsibilities as mother, friend, confidante, wife, caretaker, baby-sitter, etc., plus the responsibilities you have at work during a given day or week, probably mean that you wear more hats than you ever thought possible. You are a *multi-person*. You experience many shifting identities and take on several roles at once. There's nothing pathological about this label. The realities of twenty-first century life necessitate that women and men, and even teens and children, operate in many worlds, in many capacities, in different spaces.

It's the nature of our fast-paced, highly accelerated, high-tech planet. There are so many "social selves" and ways of being, so many people in so many situations, that you can lose your sense of who you really are. You can easily slip into an identity crisis because you are so "out there"—your attention so focused outside—that you lose track of the true you. You begin to wonder, "Who am I?" and "Why am I so confident and self-assured at work and so wimpy and unassertive at home?"

You've probably become adept at morphing from a mom into a manager—seeing your children off to school and then tackling the responsibility for overseeing twenty employees. You're an online investor one moment, a weekend chef another. But these roles are superficial, and they are a relatively easy component of managing tasks in complex times. The challenge of the brave woman is to shift roles and identities while keeping your essential self intact and, despite rapidly shifting circumstances, maintaining your bravery.

Robin, a veterinarian in her thirties, said: "I can do anything at work. In our practice, I specialize in large animals, cattle, sheep, horses, goats. I am fearless when it comes to handling sick horses and sheep—giving them injections, pulling their teeth, even putting them down when necessary. I'm brave when I'm trekking. I've hiked all over the world and even worked at one of the field stations below Mount Everest for a few months. But when it comes to men and my relationships, I'm a wimp and a coward."

Time and time again, women reveal their fears and the bravery it takes to overcome them. Robin's assessment of her "split personality" regarding her guts and courage is quite common.

Barbara, for instance, is a fearless and confident performer. She is relaxed and comfortable while directing a large choral group or while playing jazz in a piano bar. If you tell her, however, that she must give up her apartment and move to a different city, the mere thought of it creates jitters and causes her palms to sweat.

The fear of change, such as Barbara's fear of relocating, is one of the great obstacles to success. If you allow it to, however, your bravery can move you past it. Change is always difficult. It threatens your stability; it threatens the known with the unknown. Change

brings out your worst feelings about failure ⟨
even be viewed as a threat to your basic existe.

Although your fears may seem like an exag⟨
ings on which they are based have a long history.
were created at a time when you were powerless an⟨
infant with few resources, totally dependent on your pa
caretakers for your survival and existence. Childhood en⟨
nite in the present, particularly in situations that require ⟨ning
different from us, circumstances that require risk, change, learning a
new skill, dealing with an untried environment, learning untested
ground rules in unfamiliar territory.

Be Brave in Every Facet of Your Life

Most women are brave in several parts of their lives. However,
few stand up or assert themselves in both their careers and relationships and with their families. At home, a woman may be a take-
charge dynamo, running the family finances, caring for the children
and her husband, keeping track of family appointments, etc. At
work, that same dynamo may be reticent to take charge of a work
project or reluctant to express her suggestions and ideas.

Many women are uncomfortable with power: the power to
influence people and situations, the power to have your agenda lis-
tened to and acted on, the power to change circumstances, etc. Other
women find themselves reversing their roles: becoming aggressive at
work and reticent at home, or a "wuss" at work and controlling in
romance.

Lina, a writer in her twenties, said: "I'm not afraid of external
things, it's my internal weirdness that's hard to face down. What I
mean is not having the will to complete goals, being afraid of writing
something shitty, and therefore not writing at all. My issue is inertia.
There are certain things I don't put enough power toward. So I usually write some kind of document (this is the math geek in me) that
helps me organize my thoughts and fears. I categorize them, then
rank them. Of course, I've kept a journal since I was twelve and have
found that writing down my fears and prioritizing what I have to do
puts me back on track."

A Journal Exercise for You

Lina's method of identifying the negative thoughts and fears
preventing her from achieving a goal, listing the steps she needs to
take to realize it, and ranking both her lists of fears and priorities,

_s concrete shape to her project and the fears that surround its completion. Is fear holding you back from writing that screenplay, completing an application to law or medical school, drawing up a business plan?

Write down all the thoughts and fears that come to mind when you contemplate beginning work on a particular goal. Now rank them in order of their "scariness" with 1 being the most intimidating and 10 the most doable.

Make a list of all the things you need to accomplish to work toward your goal. Put those tasks in chronological order. You should feel more motivated to begin your project when you have a clear idea about how to accomplish it. Begin with the first step you outlined. Complete it. When you're ready, go on to the second task, and so on. When you've finished each step, small or large, assess how you feel. In most instances, your fear will diminish as your confidence begins to soar.

At Risk in Romance

As has been well documented, women's fears commonly revolve around relationships of all kinds, but particularly around romantic or intimate relationships. This tendency, which applies to women of all kinds and capacities, is promoted in the media (chick flicks, popular magazines), but also is created by your memory of the way things are "supposed to be."

Nicki: A Brave New Path

"Women are least brave about who they really are," says Nicki, a middle-aged writer and educational administrator who has been happily married for twenty-one years. "They will open up a magazine and buy whatever someone tries to sell them, whether it be how to look, or how to be successful, or what kind of relationship to have."

Nicki's greatest fear, and the only major one she can identify, is abandonment, which she claims she has had all her life. "I fear being totally alone and that comes from the time I was two, two and a half years old, and my mother was suffering from a depression that put her on Valium. I would lie in my crib and hear her tell someone else to pick me up or feed me. She couldn't move from her bed." Her older sister and brother became Nicki's surrogate parents and her sister especially tried to shield her baby sister from her parents' conflict.

Nicki experiences abandonment fear as a "palpable, real, visceral emotion. It's very scary." This fear, coupled with her father's unpredictable and erratic behavior, colored Nicki's own posture with the men she dated. She was very clingy, possessive, trying to over-please, and be ever vigilant. "I was always the one more in love. Looking for that one man who would never leave me."

Nicki's tendency to closely monitor her environment came from her father—a man who would be sane one minute and a madman the next. "I was always waiting for the next shoe to drop and taking stock of every situation. Trying to control my environment and failing to make it perfect."

When her father died sixteen years ago, Nicki decided to take control of her fears. "I realized that I could go back to school if I wanted and he couldn't do a damned thing about it. I had always focused on other people's needs. Now, I started thinking of myself, and giving me the attention I was always giving to others." When Nicki married a man ten years older than she is, her abandonment fears returned. This time she sought counseling, a process she calls "the bravest thing I've ever done. It takes even more courage to excavate the rubble and stay long enough to pour through that debris."

Nicki's high school classmates used to call her the "cowardly lion," because her tawny golden curls reminded them of Dorothy's animal companion in *The Wizard of Oz*. "He's now one of my favorite characters, the one I identify with. He was on a quest for courage, but he had it all along. He just didn't know he had it, but he was the one who showed more courage than all of them. Brave women manage to go inside, gather their courage, and transcend their surroundings."

Be Brave in Love

Women who tremble at the thought of abandonment, who will do anything to preserve intimacy, no matter what it costs them, base their relationships on irrational fears, not bravery. The brave woman knows that if fear is her prime motivator for conducting her relationships, she will lose power, and she puts her identity at risk. The greatest power in your life is consistency. Be brave in business. Be brave in love.

Dr. Barbara Kerr (1997), who has conducted extensive research and written about gifted women and girls, concludes that when it comes to relationships, so-called gifted or very smart women are particularly susceptible to the fears, traps, and pitfalls of romance culture and the false expectations it breeds. Smart women, she believes, approach romance in the same way they tackled school, their careers, and work. They want to be best in the class, and they think that an "A" in romance means attracting and marrying a man who is handsome and will take care of them.

Kerr explains: "The right kind of guy in society's eyes is often the wrong kind of guy for most gifted women, who seem happiest with the supportive, easy-going men who seem definitely unromantic to women brought up on a diet of Cosmopolitan, best-selling novels, and Burt Reynolds movies" (259).

When it came to romance and gifted women who had achieved extraordinary success and what Kerr calls "eminence," the painter Georgia O'Keefe, the anthropologist Margaret Mead, and Katherine Hepburn all discovered their personal passion first and then love followed. Their love and work lives were inextricably entwined. The story goes that Hepburn met the great love of her life, Spencer Tracy, on the set of *Woman of the Year*. The legendary couple started out as friends and fellow actors. Later, their on-screen roles turned into a real love match that lasted over twenty-six years and through nine motion pictures they made together.

Exploration toward Bravery
Fearing Change Obliterates Bravery

One of the most important questions to consider is how fearing change affects your ability to be brave, to take charge, to take responsibility, and to make new situations happen in your life. Think seriously about this question: Everyone finds excuses not to be brave. People blame and fault-find others and themselves. They fear being outside of their "comfort zone," which ultimately leads to a diminished, less satisfying, and less fulfilling life. Do you think this possibility exists for you? If so, write in your journal how this is true and why.

By identifying on paper what your fears are regarding change, you will be more apt to stretch yourself, move out of your comfort zone more frequently, and eventually welcome interruptions to your routine and ways of doing things.

Bravery Depends on You—Not the Opinions of Others

You may fear being brave because taking control and responsibility for your life means you can make mistakes, fail, be criticized, and be disapproved of and/or rejected. Obviously, these types of fears greatly diminish bravery. Being brave is what you are despite the criticism, disapproval, or rejection of others. Once you learn to view opprobrium, opposition, and criticism differently, your bravery will allow you to adequately deal with and benefit from all of your experiences. The secret is to redefine your beliefs about failure, disapproval, rejection, and criticism. See them as pinpricks that you learn from, not as mortal wounds.

The brave new you never allows others to define who you are or what you can do. You are the one who tests yourself, defines personal success, and identifies your limits. You are the only person who accurately can do this—not others. You can weigh what people say to you by considering who they are, where they are coming from, and by evaluating whether they have the ability to place your best interests and personal growth above all else. By depending on your personal experience and inner knowing, you can discern from where the advice or opinions of others' is originating.

The Emotional Truth of Fear

Human beings are emotional creatures. For most, emotions fuel dreams and desires. However, emotions also have the ability to abruptly halt situations. You may believe that fear is an emotional signal for you to stop what you are doing. Remember, however, the brave woman forges ahead not because of the absence of fear, but in spite of it. This occurs because the brave woman understands fear differently than most people. She knows fear is an emotion from *within* not a reality from without. She knows the difference between fear that is created by forging ahead in her life and creating new possibilities, and the fear that naturally occurs when she is in imminent danger.

What about your fears? Write in your journal the fears that are holding you back. For most people, it's the fear of success, fear of failure, and fear of change. What are you afraid of losing? What's the worst thing that could happen if you succeed? What is the worst thing that could happen if you don't?

To name and label your thoughts and feelings is to make more sense of them and to understand them better. Naming and labeling allows you to have more influence. You'll feel less overwhelmed and your situations will be far more manageable than if your thoughts and emotions were silently festering inside of you. By naming and labeling your fears and other emotions you are giving yourself the permission to express the brave new you as never before.

If you have completed all the exercises in this chapter, you have cracked open and exposed the shell of fears, "the inner weirdness" that holds many people back and keeps them from achieving what they want for their lives. Identifying and coming to terms with your fears is the tough part. In the next chapter, you will discover how the many facets of your personality affect the brave new you.

Chapter 6

Make the Most of Your Personality

Maximize Your Greatest Strengths

Open your arms to change but don't let go of your values.

—The Dalai Lama

Medieval epics, Shakespeare's plays, tarot cards, soaps operas, celebrity magazines, and more all fix on the fascinating variety and dynamics of personalities. Why is it that one person will dive into the pool without getting wet first, while someone else will sit on the edge, dangle her toes in the water, and only wade in after she's tested the water temperature and found it to her liking? Why are some of you good listeners, and others require center stage most of the time? Why do you pay the bills on time, and your partner waits to the last minute? The reason is your personality. Your individual character or personality type reflects how you act, how you protect and defend yourself, and how you express your bravery.

Ancient philosophers classified plants, animals, weapons, ships, and temperaments or personality styles, a trend that continues up to the present day in the form of enneagrams, astrological charts, horoscopes, and the more scientifically based psychological profiles used by therapists.

Personality type is the key to the way you express your bravery and the circumstances that squelch it. In chapter 2, you learned that whatever happened in your past does not determine your future. You are not a "victim" of your past, but a person who can evolve and change through time. To some degree, the same is true of your personality. Dynamic strategy No. 6 is taking inventory of your personality to determine how your defining characteristics affect your destiny.

Like wine, most personalities mature and ripen with time. They evolve. You can maximize your strengths and turn weaknesses into assets by understanding what motivates you to think and act in the ways you do, by discovering how you face challenges and express your bravery, by chipping away at excuses and defenses that inhibit your bravery until you come upon the brave new you.

After reading this chapter, you'll never again say: "That's just the way I am, I can't do anything about it" or, "Nothing will change—the situation is hopeless." Instead, you'll say: "I'm going to use my bravery to break through the barriers and limitations that hold me back. I'm going to take advantage of my strengths and apply them to the best of my ability to achieve my goals. I'm going to change my approach to my relationships and create greater choices and possibilities for myself. Fear no longer rules my life. I want to be bold, take risks, and be strong in the face of criticism. I'll go after what I want and what's important to me, and, in the process, become a better person for it."

Being committed and determined to change results in more than just the new accomplishments that you'll achieve. You will go through a personality transformation in the process.

Know Yourself for Success

It's important to know your strengths and weakness to set yourself up for success and minimize failure. Think of a few words that describe your personality, such as: adventurous, self-confident, changeable, impulsive, artistic, solitary, serious, bold, cautious, devoted, sensitive, dramatic, vigilant, energetic, bubbly, domineering.

Notice that in typing a personality, we use one word to characterize a whole pattern of attitudes and behaviors that label a person across a broad spectrum of situations and predicaments. In other words, it's the general or overall "flavor" of a person that sticks in our mind and allows for these characterizations or personality types.

What Is Personality?

Your biology, your genetic makeup, and the environment in which you grew up are major factors in determining who you are and how you relate to the world and people in it. Your personality also shapes how other people react and relate to you, factors that further establish and ingrain your "personality characteristics."

By this definition, *personality* is your makeup at birth molded by your life circumstances. Thus our personalities are malleable rather than fixed. However, the choice to undergo a "personality change" rests with you and in your determination and motivation. A person can be described and characterized by saying: she's outgoing or shy and reserved, or bitter, or bouncy, introverted, extroverted, creative, devoted, aggressive, dramatic, sensitive, peculiar and eccentric, suspicious. Each of us has a distinct personality, but the list of personality classifications is endless.

On a larger scale and along an even wider spectrum, your individual personality can plug into a category or group of other personalities who have similar but not identical characteristics. Keep in mind, the classification of personality types is a controversial area, because people mean different things by "personality" and there are many definitions to describe it.

Many theorists and experts on personality tend to divide personalities into three or four broad categories with subsets of three or four more types within that range. Steven K. Scott, author of *Simple Steps to Impossible Dreams: The 15 Power Secrets of the World's Most Successful People*, likens personalities to animals. He divides them into lions, otters, golden retrievers, and beavers, and enumerates the natural strengths and weaknesses of each type (81–90). Another popular personality classification system is based on the nine personality types of the enneagram, an ancient psychological system that, in turn, relies on the pioneering work of Carl Jung (Riso 1990).

Personalities of a Lifetime

Some people believe that personality is fixed from childbirth, and no matter what a person experiences or what insight they have about themselves, their personality never changes—what you see is truly what you get. Others believe that people have the capacity to change "permanent behavior" through dedication to self-growth and personal expansion. The premise of *Brave New You* is based on this latter theory.

You will *evolve* or "grow up" into the person you want to become by learning about your behavior patterns, including how you cope and react, what you expect from others, and how you handle stress. Additionally, your personality is defined by:

- How you view the world. Do you see your environment as a safe and nurturing place or is it threatening and unsafe?

- How you present yourself, i.e., what is your impact on your environment?

- How you make decisions.

- How you routinely do things.

- How you protect yourself from pain and hurt.

The Benefits of Knowing Your Personality

Your personality comes through in how you experience yourself and the way others view you, in the way you communicate with others, how you express your attitudes, in the way you think, what you feel, your actions, what you dream, and how you interact and deal with others.

Knowing your personality allows you to see:

- What motivates you.

- Your communication style.

- How you define your boundaries.

- Your decision-making process.

- What part fears play in your life and how they are expressed.

- How you relate to others and how others relate to you.

- How you respond to stress, change, and conflict.

- What success and failure mean to you.

- How much of a risk-taker you are.

- What part security plays in your life and how it's expressed.

- Your emotional sensitivity.

- What drives you.

- What is important and meaningful to you.

Personalities in Style

Transforming your personality requires the energy of bravery. Moreover, as you gain awareness of your personality "traits," you will inventory the qualities that promote your well-being as well as the qualities that hold you back and stifle your initiative.

Predictable Decisions or Spontaneous Choices?

For example, you may have noticed that you are a "planner," someone who is methodical and must have everything in place in order to take action. You gather and weigh the facts about a situation before making a decision on anything of importance. The challenge for you is to understand that sometimes things don't always go according to plan. Your courage comes from balancing your natural caution by pushing through without having everything perfectly in order.

The flip side is the person who makes quick decisions with minimal information. She appears to be "impulsive," at least by a planner's standards. She's out of the gate before she barely settles in the saddle. As soon as she hears the gun, she's off. The challenge for her is to hold back, pull in the reins, and become more deliberate in the way she approaches things.

Perhaps you are the kind of person who craves variety, excitement, and unpredictability. You love that feeling of never knowing what's going to happen next—a "living by the seat of your pants" style that would be unnerving to someone who yearns for predictability, consistency, and security, and certainly unsettling to a person who doesn't like surprises. To balance these tendencies, try sticking to a routine for a week or plan an outing and put all the details in place before the event.

Socializing with Others or Hanging Out Alone?

You may have a personality that's very people oriented. What you value most is a good time with people, preferring activities that best express your "extroversion." You are invited to many social gatherings, because you can be counted on to be the life of the party and you never disappoint. For the gregarious people-person extrovert, spending time alone becomes boring very quickly and even makes her lonely. Being completely alone with only her own thoughts is prison for the people-oriented extrovert. To balance this fear, people-person extroverts need to become comfortable spending time alone and in contemplation.

On the other hand, you may cherish alone time. You prefer solitary activities or small infrequent gatherings. Your introverted style and introspective type derives the greatest satisfaction spending hours on a pet project, or working on your novel, limiting the "distractions" from others in order to think and be creative. For the more introverted, introspective, solitary woman, alone time is an escape from the chaos of everyday living with its unending intrusions and interruptions. She loves to sit and watch the waves roll into shore or hike alone in the woods. Her bravery gets exercised when she must put herself "out there" in public or social situations.

The Orientation of Personality

Your personality not only has a style, but also an *orientation* or general outlook. Personality orientation, which has nothing to do with political affiliations or sexual preferences, is defined by an attitude and behavior that can change and is shaped by the various experiences and events of your life.

A Pioneer or a Preservationist?

Two common personality orientations are the "pioneer," who is liberally oriented, and the "preservationist," who is more conservatively oriented.

If you're a pioneer, you need to have variety in your life. You're comfortable if the "loose ends" aren't tied up. It's not important if you don't see a beginning, middle, and end to situations. You prefer spontaneity to anything predetermined. You prefer a fluid, flexible schedule, not a "rigid" one. Since creative expression is more important to you than the ground rules for expressing it, it isn't important for you to have crossed all your *t*'s and dotted your *i*'s. Besides, in your universe, ground rules should be bendable—and can be broken—should the situation warrant it.

As a pioneer, you have a "live and let live" approach to life. What others find strange or bizarre, you see as intriguing or fascinating. A nine-to-five work schedule stifles you. Given a choice, you prefer the unconventional to the conventional. Novelty is more important for you than predictability and sameness. You prefer the arts, self-expression, and self-direction, rather than following someone else's path. You prefer to do what you think rather than what you're told.

You crave adventure, new experiences, and new situations. You enjoy experimentation. As a "free spirit," you would rather not be bogged or weighted down by the encumbrances of an inflexible society telling you what to do, how to do it, and when to do it. You'd rather break new ground than tread the old one. You gain inner guidance more from your own self-reflection than from hearing it from someone else. You are intuitive, relying more on what you feel and on your hunches than on purely cerebral or logical information.

Conversely, if you are a preservationist, you value power and tradition. You like routine and you don't mind following directions, especially if you are asked to do something by someone you respect or someone in a position of authority. More conforming than your pioneer counterpart, you believe in rules, and you trust that regulations allow for smooth functioning and keep society from lapsing into chaos. If you are more a conservative preservationist, you consider orderliness and predictability essential to your day-to-day functioning.

You are conscientious and possess a highly developed sense of right and wrong. The preservationist wants predictability. In fact, surprises can be unnerving and upsetting for her. Schedules, routines, family customs, and traditions are important to you. You love details and are methodical, exhaustive in the way you apply yourself to problems. The preservationist has everything under control. You are accurate, analytical, and extremely focused.

One personality orientation or style is not better than the other. Differences in personality make for a "creative tension" within each individual. It's the classic duel between Apollo and Dionysus, the part of you who waits for the right moment and the part that wants to "seize the day" this moment. One personality orientation or style counterbalances the other. To have one style to the exclusion of the other is to invite disorganization, and lessens the potential to make changes. Excess in either direction is an invitation to weaken the human spirit and shut down the power of a woman's bravery.

The Fifteen-Minute Personality Test

Listed below are one hundred personality traits that each of us experience to one degree or another. To help you understand what traits dominate your personality and form a larger constellation or character type, we have divided the traits into three common personality clusters: the dependent character type; the controlling character type; and the competitive character type. Place a checkmark next to all of the personality traits that typify your thoughts and behavior.

Constellation One: The Dependent Character Type

____ It's important for me to feel loved.

____ I need to feel secure in my job.

____ I am reliable and a hard worker.

____ My friends and family can count on me.

____ I don't express my pain or hurt readily.

____ I continually need reassurance.

____ Some of my family and friends call me "mother earth."

____ It takes a lot for me to become angry.

____ I need confirmation that I am lovable.

____ I need another person to feel complete.

____ I fuss a lot when someone I love is sick.

____ I am extremely sensitive to abandonment and rejection.

____ I am extremely agreeable, even if I don't want to be.

____ I am conservative in my lifestyle.

____ I don't like change.

____ I go along with others.

____ I need support to take action.

____ I don't like to be alone to exercise, shop, or travel.

____ I want to know where my partner is and with whom.

____ I don't like to spend time alone.

____ I'm a great listener.

____ I give my friends a lot of time and empathy.

____ I tend to tune out reality.

____ I like peace at any price.

____ I know how things should be and try to model my life on that.

____ I believe things will always take care of themselves.

_____ I never do anything that would cause someone else pain or harm.

_____ I care what others think.

_____ When someone treats me badly, I minimize the hurt.

_____ I like to tell others about my life and problems.

_____ My idea of being happy is to feel secure.

_____ I expect others to rescue me from predicaments.

_____ I am extremely generous even if others don't reciprocate.

_____ I think giving is more important than receiving.

_____ I expect others to acknowledge my generosity.

Constellation Two: The Controlling Character Type

_____ I value my thoughts and opinions.

_____ I am very conscientious.

_____ I possess a deep sense of right and wrong.

_____ I am rational and pride myself on not being "emotional."

_____ I am moderate and think situations through.

_____ I like to work alone and find it difficult to collaborate on a project unless I direct it.

_____ I start working on my income taxes right after New Year's.

_____ I am excellent at planning parties.

_____ I am very task-oriented and try to complete one project at a time.

_____ I work slowly but accurately.

_____ I am a precise and factual communicator.

_____ I am especially focused on the details.

_____ I need to gather a lot of information before making a decision.

_____ I try to avoid tense situations.

_____ I operate best in a conflict-free environment.

____ I don't take many big risks.

____ I balance my checkbook as soon as I write a check.

____ Some people say I have strong opinions.

____ I am very well organized.

____ At times I can be a perfectionist.

____ I receive tremendous pleasure from working hard.

____ I can be judgmental.

____ I like to be in control of a situation.

____ I'm the best judge of my life.

____ I don't express my feelings very much.

____ I like to explain my actions in great detail.

____ Sometimes I want to do something, but I don't dare.

____ I keep my impulses in check.

____ I find it difficult to say, "I love you."

____ My greatest fear is being proven wrong.

____ I should watch out for criticizing other people.

____ I see the trees rather than the forest in many situations.

Constellation Three: The Competitive Character Type

____ I am very good at presenting ideas to others.

____ Status and prestige are important to me.

____ I like being a winner.

____ I am extremely pragmatic.

____ Coworkers call me the "concept person."

____ I'm always the first one to jump in the pool.

____ My physical appearance is "unconventional."

____ I am goal-oriented.

____ I am anxious to prove myself.

____ Tennis and chess are a couple of my favorite pastimes.

____ I can be chameleon-like.

____ I must admit, I'm more concerned with style than substance.

____ I often feel special.

____ I have problems with intimacy at times.

____ I want everyone to accept me for who I am.

____ Others are jealous of me.

____ I have a lot of energy.

____ Other women seem to compete with me.

____ I want to be famous one day.

____ I never want to grow old.

____ Growing up I was always trying to best my siblings.

____ I brag about my accomplishments sometimes.

____ I fall in and out of love very quickly.

____ I have a rich fantasy life.

____ Flattery will get you everywhere with me.

____ I like it when people give me compliments.

____ I want people to take notice of what I do.

____ I am aware of how I look most of the time.

____ I am always aware of the way others look at me.

____ I don't express my feelings directly.

____ I am always trying to prove something.

____ I seem very confident and self-assured even though I may not be.

____ Sometimes I think I should have been an actress.

Now add up how many traits you checked off in each constellation. Were most of your checkmarks in constellation one, two, or three?

Are You Loyal and Lovable?

If you checked off fifteen or more of characteristics in constellation one, there is no doubt you tend toward the dependent character type. At your best, you are a loving, independent, successful, and well-liked woman. You are easy to talk with, naturally giving, and a real nurturer. You bring out the best in others by providing support and empathy. You are intuitive and accept other people's flaws and points of view. Others come to you for advice and for a shoulder on which to cry. Passionate, warm, sincere, friendly, you believe in the causes that are important to you. You make a good mediator, and an excellent teacher or therapist. You excel at public relations or running a business involving the public.

Of all the character types, you possess the greatest capacity to love others. In relationship, you support your partner's growth and changes. On the downside, you are the most likely personality to be a victim. You may wallow in helplessness and expect others to rescue you. You fear abandonment and prize security. Being alone terrifies you because you only feel complete by being with another person. You are devastated when you find out that others don't like you. Being loved and liked is of primary importance to you. You are loyal to a fault and tend to agree with others to preserve intimacy.

The Challenges

Many times you express hurt, anger, and guilt through physical symptoms, passive-aggressiveness, or by displacing these emotions onto a child, even an animal. You will tend to overprotect your family, and "baby" or "mother" others. You call your loved ones several times a day and panic if they become ill.

At her most dysfunctional, the dependent character wants to be treated like a queen, but will tolerate gross abuse. The most common and controversial constellation, its characteristics seem gender-based.

Bravery in Action

The bravest actions you can take:

- Spend time alone.

- Travel on your own.

- Speak your mind even if it means being criticized.

- Release your emotions.

Do You Like to Run the Show?

If you have checked off fifteen traits in constellation two, you probably fit into the controlling character type, a constellation shared by Martha Stewart, Barbra Streisand, Heloise, and many other high-powered women. The natural traits of these personalities fit extremely well with what they do in life. These women have discovered perfect outlets to maximize their strengths and capitalize on their weaknesses in work that demands attention to detail and a desire to run the show on a movie set, in the home, or in the boardroom. This personality makes excellent advance people, conference organizers, archaeologists, charity organizer, art curator, accountants, bankers, physicians, and film directors.

At your best, you are decisive and authoritative without being judgmental. You support others' projects financially as well as intellectually. You can pick apart any project, see all sides of the issues, and temper your suggestions for improvement with kindness and understanding. In relationships, you allow yourself to become vulnerable and have learned to be more spontaneous in your lovemaking. You let others learn from their mistakes and don't try to correct or impede their growth. You can admit you need other people and that you can make mistakes and that's all right.

The Challenges

Your greatest fear is being condemned for your beliefs. Some of you concoct stories to cover up your disappointments and hurts. You minimize your pain and find it very difficult when it comes to expressing either love or any negative emotion. You have the potential to become a perfectionist. On the other hand, you can't stand others' imperfections. You can, as the saying goes, "dish it out." But you take criticism badly and rarely forget or forgive a slight or personal injury.

Bravery in Action

The bravest actions you can take:

- Admit you're wrong.

- Make a mistake intentionally.

- Loosen up, and let go.

Your goals are to become more spontaneous, less rigid, take pleasure in the moment, break some rules, carpe diem, forgive and forget, and look at the big picture.

Do You Always Go for the Gold?

If you checked off fifteen or more traits in constellation three, you are most probably the competitive personality type. You are driven, inquisitive, and dynamic in your style. You want to be the best in every area of your life and put your mark on the world.

Those of you who fall into the competitive character type have a superb capacity for social interaction. Because of your charm and charisma, people are drawn to you naturally.

The Challenges

You adapt to people and change your personality easily. You are a chameleon and risk losing your core. Your challenge is to be self-accepting and not act out. You fear being embarrassed, laughed at, made fun of, or made to look silly. Perhaps you're an imposter, you think, who has gotten to this place on a fluke.

As you meet your challenges and move toward bravery, you will feel more equal and accepting of others. You will look behind the surface of people and things and expand your awareness of your own depth as well as others. You will live in the real world not some fantasy of your invention. And, instead of running away from your emotions or leaving a relationship without working on it, you will acknowledge and experience your feelings.

Bravery in Action

The bravest actions you can take:

- Be more honest with others and yourself.

- Work on developing an inner life.

- Try to become collaborative and cooperative with others.

- Watch for others who play to your blind spots or use flattery to get what they want from you.

- Love yourself, not the false image you present to the world.

Natural Strengths and Weaknesses

Each personality type has natural strengths and weaknesses. Minutes after you are born, you're expressing both endearing and not so appealing qualities about yourself—your personality traits.

Your parents and other family members are the best gauge for describing you as a baby. Looking back, they may say that you were easygoing and not a problem. That you slept through the night, were trouble-free to nurse, obedient, never cried much, and were sensitive and happy most of the time. Or they describe you as strong-spirited, stubborn, and irritable. You made your needs known rather forcibly—they saw you as a handful, even before the world had an impact on you.

Find one of your baby pictures and study it. What is the expression on your face? Is it placid, pouting, defiant, happy? Find out if your parents kept a baby book or journal. What did they write about you?

It's very important to take a long hard look at your "personality." This process can be difficult and it takes a great deal of your courage, but it is crucial in promoting your growth and changes—an essential element in understanding yourself and your impact.

Take note of the strong qualities of your personality, then cultivate and strengthen them. Notice the qualities about yourself that are not in your best interest and could hurt and hinder you in your relationships and in your present and future opportunities. Be on guard when your self-talk tells you that you can't change your deep-rooted characteristics. You may say to yourself, "This is the way I am and have always been." Meaning "This is the way I'll always be, I'll never change." Negative, self-defeating beliefs like these come from your ideas about yourself and others, and a society that tells you it can't be done.

The truth is it can be done—if you have the courage to face yourself honestly, without pretense. The rewards from your inner work and exploration will be very liberating for you.

What Is a Personality Disorder?

Sigmund Freud zeroed in on the pathological or disease aspects of personality and fathered what are now called *personality disorders*. The difference between a personality and a personality disorder is a matter of degree and intensity.

A personality disorder is actually a personality trait that becomes rigid and inflexible. The personality becomes exaggerated and interferes with someone's ability to live a happy and self-empowered existence. A personality trait becomes a disorder if that trait impedes your happiness, relationships with others, capacity for self-fulfillment, work, creativity, or social life. If you find that your personality is interfering with your life, it would be wise to seek counseling for your problems.

Changing a Personality

You probably recognized yourself in one or all of the three personality constellations and can pinpoint the areas where you need to become braver. You'll need to work diligently at this strategy. The process will not be rapid. Your personality is a part of you and the essence of what makes you who you are. Think of your personality as a magnificent but still unfinished piece of sculpture, a work-in-progress that you continuously shape, mold, and polish.

Time and experience can create personality changes in people with little conscious effort. Typically, however, personality changes require focus, and they don't happen overnight. They do happen, however, if you're committed to what you want and if you stoke your desire with the flames of bravery.

Chapter 7

Live Up to What You Believe In and Do What's Important to You

I make the decision over and over again, every day,
to stand up for what I know to be true.

—Judy Chicago

Becoming a brave woman requires a great deal of soul-searching. Part of that soul-searching is to know at any given time what is truly important to you and what your life mission and purpose are. You may think you know what's important and what you believe in, but look closer and you'll discover that what was once vital and meaningful to you has most probably changed over time and with life-transforming events.

During critical turning points, you may experience unease or even upheaval. You may feel these emotions subliminally or tell yourself "there must be more." You might become upset or confused, because you "have it all" and are doing the things that are supposed to bring you happiness. But why don't you feel happy?

You may begin to think there's something's wrong with you. Do you chastise yourself for being ungrateful for what you have? Do you experience guilt that comes from questioning your good fortune?

The good news is you've changed. Your experiences and shifting responsibilities have unsettled and moved the earth around you. What was once so dearly important, no longer is. What you never entertained as being important begins to loom larger and takes center stage. At any age, it takes courage to go back to ground zero and see what you feel and think about your priorities now. As a brave woman, this type of soul-searching and reevaluating is what you must do if life is to make sense and have genuine meaning.

Dynamic strategy No. 7 is to discover your life's mission, to define your priorities, and to find out what's really momentous to you. There is a Native American proverb that asks: *Can you stand in the middle of the fire and not shrink back*? Can you answer yes to this challenge? Can you identify your values and beliefs? Do they line up with your current goals and lifestyle? Achieving and maintaining clarity is the precursor to lasting self-confidence and the bravery needed to pursue your passions and genuine ambitions.

Focus on Your Priorities and Life's Mission

Beliefs are mental and emotional commitments that are essential to you. Values entail acting on your beliefs. Do things differently and you experience freshness in your life. This requires the courage to plan, dream, and take action. It starts with your bravery. Until you decide to exercise the bravery within, you won't move forward in your quest to fulfill your dreams and ambitions, sometimes dreams and ambitions you never dreamed that you even had.

Judy Johnson, a prize-winning poet and grandmother, recently took up skydiving and now spends her free time leaping out of an airplane. She's become a hero to her poetry students. Judy is living proof that it's never too late to fly.

The Inspiration of Heroes

Heroes are inspiring because their ideals and beliefs are transparent. You know where they stand and you are aware of what they believe in. You find yourself naturally gravitating to heroes who best represent your values and what is most important to you.

When you live your dream, your heroes reflect the dream that has become your reality. Despite setbacks and adversity, heroes support and encourage you to live your dreams. If you yearn for something more, you will be attracted to heroes who represent your future. If you are not clear what you want and where you are going, a good yardstick is to take an inventory of the kinds of people who peak your interest and about whom you are naturally curious. They will exemplify what you want for yourself.

Heroes as a Mirror to Yourself: An Exercise

In your journal, or on a special sheet of paper, make a list of who your heroes are right now. In another column, make a list of who your heroes have been in the past.

You can gauge how much you (and maybe even society) have changed—in your views, in what's important to you, in your values—by noticing how you have changed heroes. Heroes once important may have lost their allure and may no longer be as interesting or compelling. Now new heroes have attracted your attention, some you hadn't before noticed. They command our attention because of our changed circumstances and changed awareness.

Doris Day: A Brave New Path

At the Cypress Inn, a small hotel co-owned by Doris Day, golden retrievers and cocker spaniels are greeted on arrival with biscuits and special beds, and during their stay, share the front lobby with incoming guests and passersby. Hotel rules maintain that animal guests are never to be left alone in their rooms. Pet-sitting services are provided when owners find it necessary to be out on their own.

The inn reflects Doris Day's attitudes and beliefs about animals and how they should be treated and protected. These attitudes may seem a little quirky to some people, but standing up for helpless animals and making their fate and well-being her priority is now one of Doris Day's passions and life work. This actress-singer is an icon who eschews the celebrity label and acts on her beliefs and values. And she has the courage to pull it off. Her most prominent role today is advocate for animal rights. Doris Day knows what's important to her.

Since the early seventies when Doris Day founded her Pet Project, she has used her celebrity to lobby on behalf of animals and to bring about the needed reforms to protect them. Her original project turned into the Doris Day Animal League and its sister organization, the Doris Day Animal Rights Foundation, whose missions are to advocate protecting animals and educating the public about animal protection issues. Current projects are to educate judges and prosecutors about the compelling link between animal abuse and violence toward humans, and to find creative solutions to problems such as pet overpopulation.

Doris Day has been up front about her compassion for animals. Her activities are so public, in fact, that her detractors are more than willing to tell her about her misplaced priorities and how she should spend her time and energy. It doesn't matter, because Ms. Day acts from a place within her that speaks for her courage and her passion. She knows what she believes in, she knows what she must do and does it.

Prioritize to Maximize Your Choices

Women's aspirations vary tremendously. For some, a high-profile career and affluent lifestyle are crucial to their sense of fulfillment. Other women discover that being a mother and having a job close to home win out over a career on the fast track. You can't have it all, but you can sure have a lot. You can have enough to make your life rich with adventure, purpose, and meaning. You can have more than you have now, if you so desire.

Today women have multiple choices and have the ability to mix and match careers with personal lives. Women choose to work all the time, full-time, part-time, and before, during, and after having children. They work at home, in an office, on the road, or a combination of all three. They choose to get married or to remain single. They choose to cohabit with a significant other. They choose to be married and not to have children. Or they choose to have children and not to be married.

With rare exception, your priorities determine your choices. Priorities also depend on your values, what's most important to you, and on the makeup of your personality. Setting priorities in a conscious, deliberated way is a crucial part of being brave. Your values and personality mutually reinforce your priorities. Your personality and values, however, are not fixed. You can and do change: you grow older, or you become more willing to take risks, or your children leave home and go out on their own, or you get divorced or become widowed. As you change, your values shift.

Elizabeth Norman: A Brave New Path

Elizabeth (Beth) Norman is a wife and mother, a best-selling author, an associate professor, and director of New York University's doctoral program in nursing. Her latest book, *We Band of Angels* (1999), tells about the brave nurses who banded together and defended their patients in World War II. Beth, when faced with multiple tasks that all require enormous reserves of time and energy, literally writes down her priorities and methodically accomplishes her tasks in the order in which they correspond to her list. "When things get screwed up, it's always because my priorities are our of whack, like putting work ahead of my children. Know what's important," she counsels.

In the late Eighties, Beth had just gotten her Ph.D., she had a brand new baby, and she wanted to turn her dissertation into a book, plus she had a tenure-track job at a university. It didn't seem like she could possibly do all these things at once. Would she ever get the book done?

The first thing Beth did was to set her priorities. She decided there was no contest. Her two children, a newborn and another young son, came first. They were her top priority. The book came second because it was a short-term project and one that would enhance her chances to gain tenure in her job. Her tenure-track job came third.

"I had to be really organized and keep a tight handle on my resources," Beth said. "And it worked. I got the book done and managed not to mess up my personal and work life doing so. Right now my family comes before my career, which doesn't mean stopping work. I just can't work to the level of concentration of my colleagues whose children are grown or who have never had children."

Beth is what psychologists called an inner-directed person. That is, she lives from and follows what she calls her "internal code." "If I were to bend to outside pressure I wouldn't be doing what I'm doing now. I'd be doing clinical work, because I was told that the research I wanted to do wasn't 'the right research.' I love what I'm doing. Passion is a very big motivation for me, so my decisions are internal."

Beth's centeredness comes from having grown up in a family that provided a strong foundation and what she calls a "consistent" personal life as an adult. Listening to Beth might convince you that she was always courageous and self-directed, but as a teenager, in a blue collar, mid Sixties community, "girls weren't encouraged to do anything," she said. "Now fifteen years later, I wonder what would have happened if I'd ever entertained the notion that I had choices. Back then, you could be a nurse, a teacher, a nun, or a secretary. And everything except the nun was an occupation meant to tide you over until you got married."

Beth's priorities are clear: her family comes first, her creative passion ranks second, her professional life third, and so on. Identifying and ordering your priorities will tell you who and what you love, what you love to do, what excites you, and what motivates you to take action. Prioritize the small things each morning and you will lend order to your day. Prioritize the three or four most important essentials in your life and you see where you and your future stand.

Follow Your Bliss and True Passions

Becoming brave and going after your dreams requires intensity, focus, and, most emphatically, passion—a consuming energy that keeps you fighting for what you want and impels you never to give up. Some people are lucky enough to be born passionate. Everything they do is charged with drive and passion. Early on, these fortunate few know exactly what fires their imaginations. They want to become a scientist and work in a lab, or follow in the footsteps of a great anthropologist, design lofts and other exciting urban spaces, anchor the news, start an Internet company, and so on. Others are born knowing their true passions, but take a circuitous route to get to them, only to come back to a long-term calling later on. Sometimes, as in the case of civil rights' icon Rosa Parks, a lifelong passion emanates from a single act of bravery.

Steven Scott (1998), who has worked with many high-profile achievers, writes that all of them exhibit tremendous zest and passion for what they are doing. Scott concludes: "People who are born with passion are as rare as plutonium." The rest of us, he suggests, must "'catch it,' much as you might catch a cold. The other way is to 'develop it,' taking specific steps to bring it into a particular area of your life where you want to achieve your dreams" (260). Once found, your passion will fuel your desires and shape your goals.

The late comparative mythologist Joseph Campbell coined the now familiar dictum: "Follow your bliss." Campbell, like all great teachers, encouraged his students to "go where your body and soul want to go. When you have the feeling [bliss], then stay with it, and don't let anyone throw you off."

From the time he was a little boy, Campbell was moved by the power of world mythology and consequently spent a lifetime studying, writing, and teaching about myths common to all cultures and people on earth. Well into his eighties, Campbell spent hours and hours at Skywalker Ranch advising George Lucas on mythological dimensions of the *Star Wars* films.

Your bliss is your passion, the external manifestation of your inner vision and fire, and the love that can last a lifetime. Bliss is always a personal matter, embedded deep in your gene pool at the cellular level and related to your true purpose in life. Whatever "floats your boat" (as the saying goes) just clicks and resonates with your soul at a primal level. You can be "turned on" by music, atoms, fiction writing, marathon running, set design, psychology—it doesn't matter. The brave woman pursues her bliss if she knows what it is; if she doesn't, she never gives up until she finds it.

Timeless Pleasure: Questions toward Passion

How do you find your bliss or true passion? You know you're passionate about an idea, a profession, a project when it is so absorbing and personally grabbing that you lose track of time pursuing it. Following your bliss doesn't feel like work, it feels like pure pleasure. While pursuing your passion, you put up with and push through the hard parts, never doubting the process, as you move toward the realization of your innermost desires.

Without intellectualizing or judging your thoughts, write down what you love to do more than anything else. Is it connected with a passionate dream or dreams that you've held for a long time? Is it easy for you to identify your passion? Are you following your bliss right now? Do you have a clear picture of yourself following your bliss or achieving that goal? Your bliss and your passion form your values and shape your life's mission.

Your Life's Mission

Your life's mission has nothing to do with whether you've chosen to be a traditional career woman, one half of a dual-career couple, a single career woman, a home worker, or a single working mother. More sweeping, more far-reaching than a career choice, your life's mission is your personal philosophy—the unique blueprint for the way you want to conduct your life and how you want to be as a person. It involves how you envision and enact your talent, your true passion, and what you believe.

Your life's mission is what fires you up with drive and determination. It comes from your values: your passionate ideas and ideals. They're personal. They're not values you imbibe from the media or from societal pressure; rather, they are the ideas you live by, the ideas that get into your bones, the ideas you can't deny.

Having a mission takes courage. In pursuing your mission, you have made a decision, and are committed to your cause. Suddenly, you are taking responsibility for fulfillment in your life. It's your plan, designed by you and not by others. It may be scary because you rise and fall by your own decisions and actions. As a brave woman with a mission, you join forces with others who have shaped the world into a better place.

Rosa Parks: A Brave Path

The idea of freedom was compelling for Rosa Parks, one of the brave women of the twentieth century. This recent Medal of Freedom honoree writes that the idea of being free impelled her to refuse to give up her seat to a white male passenger on a bus in Montgomery, Alabama, on the landmark date of December 1, 1955. This courageous act earned her the title, "Mother of the Civil Rights Movement."

In *Quiet Strength* (Parks 1994), Rosa says that she learned what freedom was from her mother, who used to tell her: "All God's children are supposed to be free." "Freedom Over Me," the song that Rosa's mother sang to her repeatedly, goes like this: "O freedom, freedom, freedom over me. And before I'd be a slave, I'd be buried in my grave, And go home to my lord and be free" (64).

Rosa recalls that these words "formed my feelings about being free. They gave me strength when things seemed bad, and they guided my thoughts about what I was willing to do to be free."

That day, when she made the choice to sit down anywhere she pleased, those words reverberating in her head prompted Rosa to decline the gentleman. "It was time for someone to stand up or sit down in my case. I just wanted to be free like everyone else. I did not want to be continually humiliated over something I had no control over: the color of my skin" (64–65).

Her single brave action determined Rosa Park's life mission: a lifelong commitment to social justice and the cofounding (with her husband) of an institute dedicated to helping youth develop their fullest potential.

Your life's mission can come from a single brave act to right a wrong or it can gradually reveal itself in time. It can derive from a burning desire, a childhood dream, from a role model, or a life-altering event.

Creating and Abiding by Your Mission: An Exercise

Companies and organizations begin with a mission or vision statement of what they're about, the values they espouse, and how they want to conduct their business. Formulating a mission statement precedes identifying organizational goals that provide more specific and precise steps for realizing the mission.

Creating a mission statement for yourself works the same way. It's a vision for your life that articulates what you're about and the values you espouse. Writing down your life's mission reinforces and concretizes your dreams.

For example, Carey's passions are filmmaking, abstract painting, and the plight of women in Third World countries. Right now she is a struggling artist who works on independent films for no pay. Her dream is to create documentary films about other struggling female artists all around the world and air her work on public television.

Carey's mission statement would read something like this:

> I, Carey Johnston, will create films for public television that document the suffering and triumphs of women artists all over the world to inspire others to pursue their artistic dreams and to feature the works of women marginalized by patriarchal cultures that otherwise would never be seen.

Carey's mission statement embodies her passions, her dream, and her values.

To create your personal mission statement, begin by making a list of your passions. Then, describe a dream or vision that incorporates your bliss or passions. What values are embodied in your dream? Identify them and write them down. Next, combine this material to create a personal mission statement that includes your passion, your dream and vision, and your values.

Congruency: Stand Up for What You Believe

In *The Moral Intelligence of Children*, Robert Coles (1998), a psychiatry and medical humanities professor at Harvard University, relates how his young students develop "moral intelligence" by studying and discussing groups such as the Pilgrims. Based strictly on their passionate values and belief in religious freedom, the Pilgrims left comfortable homes in England, risked treacherous seas, and disembarked in the American wilderness. That's real bravery. Coles bases his definition of courage on this early American example: a determination to live up to one's values and beliefs, no matter what the obstacles and difficulties, no matter what the price (120).

What distinguishes the brave woman from others is that she lives up to her values. She knows what she believes in and will fight for those beliefs even if they are unpopular, even if she is, to borrow from Henry David Thoreau, a majority of one. If you go against your beliefs, you create inner disharmony. When you stand up and express your indignation over an injustice or a hurt, you create congruency within yourself, that is, an alignment between what you think and your actions.

Creating alignment within yourself has the same effect as when your car is properly aligned. If your car's alignment is out of whack, it will swerve from right to left, unable to find the middle of the road and advance forward. The same effect happens in people: If your thoughts, values, actions, and deeds are not in sync, you tend to swerve all over the place, unable to find your center. Line up your beliefs and actions and you operate from your center. Line up your "walk" with your "talk" and you create, like Rosemary in the following vignette, a brave new you.

Rosemary: A Brave New Path

Rosemary's unwritten mission in life was always to be the best wife and mother she could be as well as a competent cook and hostess. For years, Rosemary had been playing it safe, going along with and appeasing her more conservative husband, Dave, agreeing with him on social issues and in the voting booth.

All that changed when their son Ron came to terms with his sexual identity and told his parents he is gay. Dave "hit the ceiling" and made Rosemary promise that "no one will ever know about this." At first she went along, but then she decided that keeping their "family secret" was absurd. She knew she could never change her husband's views, but she could change her own behavior. Rosemary began speaking openly about her son and his partner, John, and she voted for several "pro choice" candidates in the last election. Ironically, her marriage is "certainly stronger and more real. My children respect me, and, most importantly, I respect myself."

Stand Up for Your Rights

Standing up for your values means claiming your rights and territory. Don't let anyone steal what's yours, breach an agreement, break a confidence, or a trust. If you let someone get away with something and don't call them on it, then it's your problem. The brave woman does not allow others to take advantage of her "good graces," and defends her rights to ownership of an original idea, a project, a copyright, a trademark, a business agreement, and more.

Sarah, for example, struggled with herself for days before asserting her rights with a colleague. He had breached an agreement they had made regarding a mutual project. The project had been Sarah's baby. She had devoted three years to making it happen, first with her cofounder, then with this colleague who began working on it two years into the project. They had agreed that her name would be listed first on all official documents, and she was dismayed when she saw e-mails and letters where he had placed his name first. Although confronting him might have meant the end of their cordial working relationship, Sarah knew she must address the issue. She let a few weeks pass, so that her anger could dissipate, and then she raised the issue in a way that allowed him to save face but let him know that she meant business. The next e-mail he wrote, her name was first.

The brave woman is realistic and knows that she will not be able to correct every inequity she encounters. She chooses her battles wisely. When someone hurts her or trespasses her boundaries, however, she expresses her feelings at that moment. She makes the other person aware they are hurting her and lets them know not to do it again. The majority of people are reticent to speak out in this way, but if you don't, the offender will keep it up. Say something immediately. Don't let it pass. If you don't deal with the situation at the time it occurs (or shortly thereafter), it's very difficult to go back and recreate the offense. In addition, holding on to the hurt results in pent-up anger, which can eventually turn into full-blown depression and rage, as you will discover in chapter 8.

Write It Down: An Exercise on Assertion

Think about a time when someone tried to deprive you of your rights. It might have been as simple as someone pushing ahead of you in a supermarket line or nosing in front of your car at a tollbooth.

- How did that violation make you feel?
- Did you say or do anything about it at the time?
- Do you make a habit of asserting your rights?
- Would you say you are slightly, sometimes, or always aware of your personal space and territory?

When someone tries to own what's yours or appropriates your property, experience the full force of your emotions—the hurt, the anger, the outrage. Write about the situation in your journal, allowing all those feelings to emerge and even indulge your fantasies on paper. Decide how much time to let pass, one to three weeks is usually optimum, and then compose a few lines about how you will approach the person. Be clear and assertive, and, most importantly, factual and balanced in your approach. You have justice on your side. Many times the other person is not aware of her or his trespass and will be embarrassed or apologetic when they find out how you feel. If the move was intentional, you have flushed it out.

Weed Out What You Don't Need

As a brave woman you are very clear about your values and what you stand for. You also have *unhealthy desires,* values that are destructive to your life. You must weed them out! Not to do so will hamper and slow down your progress. It may even stop it completely.

For example, you may have the need for instant gratification. You may find yourself being impulsive, leaping before you look, and getting into trouble through unwise choices that feel good at the moment. Acting on impulse has consequences that are hurtful and can have long-range dangerous effects.

Being overindulgent with food, excessive spending, too much alcohol or drugs, or having unsafe sex are examples of following your impulses with reckless abandon, without regard to your health and safety, even the health and safety of others.

You might do things immediately, because they just feel good. Instant gratification is the value of the child, appropriate and age specific, but to be stuck with this value well into adulthood is to court failure and put you in unnecessary jeopardy.

You don't need to live a spartan existence, and absolutely you should enjoy the pleasures of life. Your most important and greatest successes and achievements, however, require time, learning, diligence, and patience.

Combat the Need for Instant Gratification: An Exercise

The first step to overcoming a "quick fix" existence is to know why and under what circumstances you become impulsive or seek instant gratification. Impulsivity comes about because you are trying to avoid unpleasant feelings or erase issues and problems you don't want to face about yourself or your relationships. The impulsive action makes you feel better in the short run, especially when you're feeling upset or out of control. Acting impulsively is foreclosing uncertainty. You want instant closure. You don't want to think things through or you want to avoid dealing with the anxiety and insecurities that come with patience and toughing it out. You want to quell your feelings and ensure they don't linger.

Impulsive behaviors also draw attention to themselves and away from the main event. For example, there may be serious problems in your primary romantic relationship. Instead of facing them, you have an affair. So the crux of the issue becomes the affair, not the marriage. The affair diverts your time and attention from problems in your relationship and is safer to deal with than its underlying causes.

Complete the following sentences in your journal:

- When I'm upset or angry, I immediately . . .

- Whenever I feel depressed or anxious, I have a strong urge to . . .

- To feel better about a bad day, I . . .

- To get even, I . . .

If your answers disclose a tendency to avoid uncomfortable feelings, start with small conscious steps toward changing your behavior. The next time you feel upset, acknowledge that you have unsettling emotions, feelings, and thoughts, and it's okay to have them. Do not avoid what you think and feel. Don't judge your feelings because then you'll have a tendency to hide or bury them, which creates the impulsive behavior in the first place.

It's important to understand that something needs to be acknowledged and addressed rather than avoided or expressed impulsively. You may feel fear and be threatened by addressing the issue. Acknowledging the truth of the matter, however, is the only way to break the cycle of impulsive behavior. You have to give yourself permission to feel the entire spectrum of responses. What you feel may often be as upsetting and disturbing as it is acceptable. Your responses signify what you feel, not who you are. Don't use these feelings to judge yourself. Use your feelings as a barometer to know that something's askew and not right with yourself or with your partner, or with your work.

Strive for Wisdom, Balance, and Temperance

The brave new you strives to make wise choices that have a positive impact on your health and well-being. As a brave woman you strive for balance and temperance, you enjoy your life to the fullest, but you think through decisions, respect yourself, and value your well-being. You realize that peace of mind, contentment, fulfillment, and the joys of your achievements come from values that express your highest potential. Values instill passion for what you do and the life that you live. You can delay gratification when necessary because you have a plan, a dream, a goal that cannot be thwarted. Your bravery and self-disciplined behavior will take you to the top. You do not overindulge in vices that hurt you.

Create Congruency of Character

As a brave woman you express impeccable *character*, the unselfconscious display of admirable qualities that others respect and find attractive. Character is a hard concept to define. It's both a moral and psychological term, close in concept to personality and reputation but more inclusive and global in relation to an individual. Reputation is less fixed than character and changes more often. Personality does not embrace the moral dimensions of character, except tangentially.

Simply put, character is the manifestation of who you are as expressed through your actions. Your character comes out in what you do, how you act toward others, and what you say. Character is also relative, especially in a culture as diverse and multifaceted as twenty-first century America.

As a brave woman, you express impeccable character by living according to your own beliefs and values. You strive for fairness in all your involvements and activities. You want others to succeed, deriving great joy from other people's successes and good fortune. You don't begrudge people anything, but serve as an inspiration and role model for others to emulate. Your energy is infectious because you know that there is so much to live for. Others entrust you with their confidences; they can rely on you to keep your word, and they know you will be fair in your dealings with them.

There are character flaws or ways of being that will detract from anyone's everyday existence and relations with others: excessive self-absorption, exploitiveness, and amorality along with the inability to empathize or imagine yourself in the other person's place. These attributes probably developed during a difficult childhood, as responses to real or psychic survival, and they are so deeply embedded in a person's psychological makeup that psychotherapy is the preferred way to deal with them.

As the brave new you, you eliminate values and behavior that hurt your character. You work on your character by constantly questioning your motives, noticing how others react to you, and monitoring how much criticism comes your way. If the criticism persists and comes from more than one individual, think about the complaints. How can you address the matter? Notice how well you listen to others' points of view. Can you listen attentively without trying to think of the next thing you're going to say? Are you flexible, tolerant in seeing another's viewpoint? Do others respect you? Are they open with you? Do they entrust you with confidences.

Asking yourself these questions and observing your behavior allow you to quantify your impact on others. Many people go through life unaware that others find them self-involved, distracted, inattentive, boring, or even tiresome. Observe your behavior while you are talking and listening. Make a mental note to estimate the percentage of time you talk and the time you listen. Observe the other person's reactions as you're speaking.

All the success in the world will not make you satisfied or happy, if you don't possess a sense of personal integrity. Speaking your mind, standing up for your beliefs and values, protecting your rights and territory, and honing your character all clear the path toward your personal happiness and success. Achieving integrity is a work-in-progress, an activity that must be worked on daily. You have made a brilliant start.

Chapter 8

Unpack Your Anger Luggage

Use Anger Energy to Supercharge Your Bravery

*How to train anger with accuracy rather than deny
it has been one of the major tasks of my life.*

—Audre Lorde

Everyone carries anger baggage: psychological duffels, backpacks, and overnight bags that are filled with personal injuries, real and imagined hurts, and memories of the way their families dealt with conflict. How you react to anger-provoking situations relates to what you've learned about handling your anger. You can learn to influence how you react to anger and rechannel its energy to empower you toward bravery.

Dynamic strategy No. 8 is to unpack your anger luggage and to begin to use anger energy to spark and supercharge your bravery and courage. As an enemy, anger distorts your perceptions and can destroy intimate relationships. As a friend, anger is the gateway to self-assertion, emotional well-being, and psychological growth and development. Experiencing, redirecting, and transforming your anger is a major component of becoming the brave new you.

In the twenty-first century, more women feel comfortable acknowledging their anger than they did in the past. Spurred on by helpful books, supportive therapists, films, and friends, women accept their anger more readily.

Still the majority of women and many men are hard-wired to think that anger is somehow "bad" or something to be avoided at all costs. Many people assume that anger is destructive and counterproductive to working out their problems and issues with lovers, family members, friends, and associates. They shy away from conflict, even though clashes and quarrels are a healthy and unavoidable part of ongoing relationships. As a consequence, women who avoid conflict experience communication breakdowns, lack of emotional intimacy, and increasing superficiality in their relationships.

Some women are uncomfortable with difficult and unpleasant emotions, so they wipe away their anger by disguising it as sadness, anxiety, sarcasm, passivity, and self-blame. Trying not to look "ugly" or seem "bitchy," controlling, or pushy, many women bury their anger and do anything to circumvent experiencing or expressing the real thing.

In reality, anger is our trumpet call to be brave—a superb messenger that tells us that someone has stepped over the line, trespassed a personal boundary, or pulled "the last straw."

No one enjoys tension and conflict, but a brave woman knows that when she faces the real issues head on and fully airs the inevitable problems, she can push through her temporary distress and find creative solutions to almost anything. Her relationships stay emotionally vital as she reduces the stress and anger that come from unresolved concerns.

The Origin of Your Anger

How we respond to anger-provoking situations depends on how we learned to react to provocations. As children, we observe our parents' anger styles: indirect backbiting, sarcasm, stony silence, out-of-control rages, even physical violence. As we get older, we take our cues from people around us and from the society at large.

Parents have a profound influence on how their daughters feel about their own anger and how they express it. Even though our mothers may be uncomfortable with their anger, they are still the yardsticks for measuring how we deal with it.

Cues from Your Mother

What did your mother do when she was angry? Did she give you that frown or look that told you how angry she was? Did she yell at you in exasperation? Did she throw things around? Was her anger measured and precise? How was she with your dad? Your siblings? Maybe you never saw her angry. The anger that you saw could have made you very frightened or it could have simply told you that your mother meant business. Your mother's anger may have never been taken seriously by anyone. Her anger style has everything to do with your own comfort level with anger and how you choose to express it.

Cues from Your Father

You can't forget your father and his anger. For men, anger is usually more up front and direct. Fathers, too, shape a woman's attitudes toward anger and establish the prevailing atmosphere in the home. Besides, male anger, much more acceptable than a woman's, is even glorified in history, in sports, and the popular media.

Was your father's anger ferocious, the kind of thunderbolt that shook the skies? Was he sulky or did he sit in stony silence? Did your dad have a temper? Did his face redden into a sunburn just before the explosion? Were you afraid of your father's anger? Was it explosive or was there ever the threat of physical violence? Your father's anger most likely had a profound effect on the way you relate to men in general, and particularly to male authority figures. You may be afraid to displease men for fear of angry retribution or live in a constant state of vigilance, always on the alert for an angry outburst. If anger was the prelude to physical discipline or even violence, you naturally would associate anger with pain and abuse. In that case, you probably try to avoid your own anger and angry feelings in others completely.

Leslie: A Brave New Path

Leslie, who remembers a family life punctuated by her father's unpredictable and explosive outbursts, would become alarmed when anyone showed anger. For years, she squelched her feelings and resolved arguments by giving in to others automatically.

After marrying a man just like her father and enduring several tension-filled years, she entered therapy to break these repetitive patterns. During role-playing sessions, the therapist would recreate her angry father, then her husband, as Leslie practiced arguing back and voicing her opinions. Gradually, her fear diminished as she learned to stand up for herself and experience the power of self-assertion.

The Lowdown on Anger

To be a brave woman is to recognize, accept, and own up to your anger. Anger is clearly a difficult and prickly emotion to experience, and even harder to admit. Many people completely bottle up their anger to preserve a self-image that makes them appear more under control than they really are. To recognize this emotion as a part of human nature can be unsettling and troubling. According to general opinion, it's not "nice" to be angry.

Anger itself, however, isn't the problem. It's what you do with it once you start to feel your face flush or become aware of that knot in your stomach. Anger will always be part of who you are. You can ignore it, minimize it, deny and submerge it so deeply within you that you fail to recognize it's there, but in the end, it remains.

The brave new you knows that you don't have to act on your anger as soon as you feel it. Instead, see it as a signal that something has happened that needs to be addressed. Someone may have made a careless remark that was hurtful and insulting. In most cases, believe it or not, the offending party usually is not even aware of having done so.

Telling people you are angry with them is not to insult them or to attack their character. It is simply conveying what you feel about the situation and why what they've said has made you angry. Anger gives you the courage to stand up for yourself when you need to, and sometimes it is the only emotion that provides you the nerve to do so. Actually, to recognize your anger brings peace of mind after you've settled down.

Rechanneled, anger can be a woman's personal trainer: it motivates her, energizes her, and gives her staying power and self-respect. Before learning nine steps to rechannel your anger (found later in this chapter), you need to know how to recognize where it hides and determine whether you suffer from anger addiction.

Are You Anger Addicted?

When some women experience fear, anxiety, emptiness, or inadequacy, they use anger to medicate themselves and temporarily dispel these feelings. Like exercising, television, telephones, caffeine, e-mail, and sex, anger can be addictive and can become a self-destructive habit when the problem goes unrecognized.

When you fail to recognize and channel anger constructively, anger itself becomes a catchall approach to managing your frustrations and misunderstandings. This will lead to trouble in the daily conduct of your affairs. If you have a "one size fits all" approach to working out your problems—that is, using the energy of anger to lash out at others and yourself in dangerous and destructive ways—then you become anger addicted.

Tina: A Brave New Path

Tina, an accomplished twenty-four-year-old actress, and Jeff, her new husband, were jetting toward Hawaii on their honeymoon. Gazing into the puffs of clouds below, Tina let her thoughts wander to that evening when she and Jeff would make love after a long hiatus. Show rehearsals, prewedding parties, and stress had left little time for real intimacy and had added ten pounds to Tina's normally thin figure.

Dinner, a walk on the beach, and kisses on the verandah fired their passion, but, once in bed, Tina noticed that Jeff was having trouble getting aroused. Instead of blaming his temporary impotence on jet lag or the alcoholic drinks the hula girls had handed him when they got off the plane, Tina assumed that she was turning him off and subtly tried to conceal herself.

"I have never been with anyone who is so self-conscious about her body!" Jeff finally blurted out as Tina struggled to cover her thighs and pulled the sheets over her breasts. His words stung, hitting her most vulnerable spots. She felt the familiar adrenaline rush, the burn of flaring nostrils, and the energy of raw anger that always swept her into full-blown rages.

By now, Tina had grabbed her robe, covered herself completely, and was working up to the kicking and biting stage. "You hate me, you hate my body, you hate your mother, you hate all women," she screamed at the top of her lungs. "You have ruined our honeymoon, and I will never forgive you for this!"

Thinking she was "sleeping with the enemy" and justified in her anger, Tina finally dozed off. Jeff wasn't Tina's adversary, anger was her enemy. By personalizing Jeff's lack of sexual response, by escalating or magnifying a minor incident into a major upset, and by hyperbolizing or exaggerating her injuries as well as his attitudes, Tina turned her honeymoon into a horror show.

Tina's tantrums snowballed during the next five years of their marriage, and sometimes her screaming grew so loud, the neighbors were forced to call the police. Jeff's words, Tina's honeymoon hurt, became the bone she unearthed and threw into many marital spats. Her constant mantra, "You never loved me," coupled with her chronic anger, distanced Jeff until he finally left—completely fed up and furious.

At a very early age, Tina had learned to "do" tantrums: kicking, biting, holding her breath, and screaming were surefire ways to grab her mother's attention from six other siblings. They made her feel important, even powerful.

Like many people, Tina didn't know how to be *mindful* about her anger. She had not learned how to read and assess her emotional overreactions or how to train her anger to make it work for rather than against her.

Tantrums discharged the buildup of Tina's anger and rage, but they failed to transform its tremendous energy and power. Instead of dealing with her emotions in a mature, courageous way, Tina would regress to a hurt little girl when angry, trapping herself and those around her in a psychological time warp.

The Masks of Anger

Anger hides everywhere. It veils itself under approval-seeking, compliance, neediness, helplessness, and depression. Suppressed anger also appears as *perfectionism*, the need to never make a mistake; *passive-aggression*, the indirect expression of anger; and *emotional numbness*, being totally out of touch with what you really feel.

Perfectionism

The compulsion to be perfect or to create the perfect environment is a common yet deceptive mask that hides anger while providing the angry woman with an illusion of control over her feelings and over events. There is a driven, hyperintense, unreal quality to this behavior, which can express itself in the need to be perfectly groomed all the time; to maintain a lawn and garden with no weeds, stray branches, or less than perfectly shaped rose bushes and trees; or to have children whose faces are always brightly polished and scrubbed and whose outfits are starched, never messy.

Lily: A Brave New Path

Before uncovering an undertow of anger and buried hostile feelings during therapy, for example, Lily would never leave her house unless she was perfectly coiffed and there were no chips in her nail polish. That manicured look was achieved by having her hair, toes, and fingernails done professionally three times weekly. Lily's closet was perfect, her refrigerator was immaculate, and she maintained her wine cellar at the perfect temperature. All this perfection didn't make Lily happy and merely concealed an angry and hurt woman. Once she dealt with her anger, Lily began to live more spontaneously. She literally let her hair down and enjoyed digging in her garden with her bare fingers.

Passive Aggression

When you're annoyed and angry with someone and you're afraid to express those feelings, or you will not own up to the anger and frustration you feel toward them, you may become *passive-aggressive*, which is when you express your anger and annoyance indirectly. This way, you are not held accountable for your anger. Passive aggression cloaks your feelings and causes you to exact revenge without recognizing it in yourself.

Anne: A Brave New Path

"I actually got angry just to feel normal," said family therapist Anne Waldorf. Because Anne couldn't always rant and rage in her therapy practice, her anger would come out in social situations as sarcasm, put-downs, and self-righteous questioning of others' behavior. At home on housecleaning days, while her husband would vacuum and she dusted and polished, Anne would deliberately pick up a speck of lint and ask if he had vacuumed yet, knowing full well that he had just put the machine away.

Coming to terms with her anger was very difficult for Anne who, as a therapist, thought she should know better. It took several years and a lot of courage to admit to herself that she had a problem. Today, having faced the problem squarely, and having attended numerous workshops on anger management, Anne is an expert on anger addiction. Her practice is built on a treatment program she designed specifically for anger addicts. "I can sense other people's anger levels very quickly," she explains. "It ekes from their pores, and colors their words and expressions. An addiction to anger or anything else takes you away from your center, the glue that holds the self together."

Emotional Numbness

Sometimes when you experience overwhelming emotions that you feel you can't tolerate, you may cut them off from conscious awareness and deny them. If these emotions continue to go unrecognized, they'll be discharged through other avenues, such as physical ailments and compulsive behavior. Numbness does have a beneficial purpose for the short term, but if your emotions remain cut off from awareness, you will experience all kinds of anxiety and panic.

Norma: A Brave New Path

Norma's anger was completely numbed out by being a compulsive runner. "It took me racing Ultra Runs (31 miles or more) to touch upon my anger," says the insurance executive in her mid-forties who began running after she survived a bout with cancer.

Norma completed the Swiss Alp Marathon by "living off the pain of climbing up and down those hills." But it wasn't until three years later, while competing in the Glacial Trail Run, that she experienced unadulterated anger for the first time in her life.

"I literally got lost during that marathon and ran nine hours and forty-five minutes. Then I started to cry uncontrollably and then I became angry. I realized that all my life I had been numbing my anger with pain. The bravest thing I've ever done is not the running, not even going through the chemotherapy, but to deal with my anger."

Since that time, Norma has worked with a therapist, engaged in extensive reading, and talked with women friends. With much emotional perseverance, Norma successfully rechanneled her anger and used the newfound energy to her advantage. She has since earned promotions at work and was made a vice president in her company. She still runs, but just for fun.

The Benefits of Therapy

The brave woman's task is to unmask her anger through self-awareness and therapy. Therapy will allow a woman to acknowledge the depth of her anger in a secure environment. Anger is not to be judged. It must be understood as an expression of hurt, due to someone's insensitivity to your wishes and needs, or to being stuck in a situation that impedes your progress and growth.

"I always get very excited when a client becomes angry during therapy," says Chicago-based psychotherapist Jenny H. Alexander. "It's a sure sign that a woman's getting healthy." She encourages patients, newly "tapped in" to their anger, to draw pictures of their fantasies and make lists of what pushes their buttons the most.

Meryl: A Brave New Path

Meryl, a top executive in a West Coast public relations firm, got in touch with what she calls her "Mr. Hyde" during a weekend retreat on the benefits of shallow breathing. Encouraged by her group leader to relax and get in a comfortable position, Meryl and the other participants exhaled in short, shallow breaths up to the point of hyperventilation. Two hours into the breathing, this normally gentle, genial lady turned into a "woman who runs with the wolves." As she visualized ripping off her boss' head and tearing his body apart limb by limb, she connected with that dark, powerful energy residing in every woman, although many times it has been deeply buried for years.

Rechannel Your Anger into Bravery

The nine suggestions that follow will teach you how to redirect and rechannel your anger, transmuting its energy to fuel your bravery into self-empowering avenues.

Reprogram the Neurons

The first step in rerouting anger is to reprogram your neurons. How you respond to anger depends on what you associate with its adrenaline surge. According to anger expert Carol Tavris (1989), "Some people learn to associate it with the positive sensations of risk, fun, vibrancy, and power. For others, that rush of epinephrine (the adrenaline hormone) signifies fear, danger, and powerlessness. The difference is a matter of attitude and experience, not raging hormones" (76).

Motivational guru Tony Robbins teaches heads of state and top athletes, such as tennis star Andre Agassi, how to link pain with self-destructive thoughts, and pleasure with positive cues. This method, called *neurolinguistic programming*, is intended to carve new pathways in the brain.

If the adrenaline rush of anger signals fear or flight for you, next time associate that feeling with thoughts and images of power, excitement, energy, and courage. Repeat that exercise until you automatically associate anger feelings with power and high self-esteem.

Find the Right Release

To redirect the energy of anger, you must find the right release. Instead of bullying, venting, or exploding away their anger, women who rechannel anger into more appropriate venues, such as meditation, weight training, or martial arts, learn additional skills and hone their bravery. Meditation teaches breathing techniques for feeling calm and peaceful and provides a space for listening to your brave self. Martial arts helps to build self-defense strategies, better define personal boundaries, improve mental discipline, and enhance emotional and physical balance. Exercise, especially weight lifting, provides a measure of your true strength and competence.

Marti and Marjorie: Brave New Paths

The ordinary stresses of marriage, motherhood, and an overwhelming amount of volunteer projects left Marti, a young mother of two in her early thirties, feeling out of control and ready to pop. "My anger felt like carbonated water in a bottle," she says. "I needed a safe way to pop that cork without taking it out on my husband or the children."

Marti began training in aikido, a Japanese martial art that originated approximately fifty years ago. The constant and repetitive standing up and falling down exhausts her anger energy when she's the attacker, while the gratification of "moving a man off his center" comes when Marti's defending herself. Physical strength doesn't determine success in aikido, where both sexes have equal footing. "Our society places so much emphasis on strength," Marti says, "and, let's face it, men have that edge with their larger bones and testosterone supply." In aikido, Marti can still control situations by redirecting her attacker's energy, a technique any woman can use in her relations with others.

Marjorie, whose ex-husband still can push her buttons even though they've been divorced for more than ten years, finds, "Chopping wood is the most satisfying release for my anger. Besides the force of hammering and the energy let off, there's that final crack that goes right through the universe—the sound connects me with everything—including myself."

Utilize Body Work

Anger settles in your jaws, teeth, neck, feet, and leg muscles, or in a network of pressure points throughout the body. Manipulating these points and massaging tightened muscles releases toxins, enhances circulation, and rechannels stored anger into energy.

Bodywork discharges blocked emotions and keeps anger and frustration from building up. Deep tissue massage, reflexology, reiki, shiatsu, mud masks, and more release accumulated emotional buildup in your muscles. Stimulating and massaging your body's muscles and pressure points also helps to disengage long-held "body" memories and allows your organs to function more efficiently.

Bodyworkers: Brave New Paths

Nantucket Island bodyworker Anne Stackhouse uses shiatsu, reflexology, and advanced skeletal work to realign the body and extract hurtful memories. "The body remembers anger connected with trauma and pain," says Stackhouse. "My work, particularly shiatsu massage, unblocks the anger in the tissues."

Another island resident, psychotherapist Sandra Cross, uses "dream work," group therapy, and pounding pillows with baseball bats to bring up anger and even rage. "When the anger starts to come out, a woman starts breathing better, feeling more. She feels her heart again, smiles, her skin looks better, her eyes are clearer. She is more who she should be."

Write Letters and Keep a Diary

For many people, writing their feelings out on paper is a powerful emotional release. Writing your uncensored thoughts each day (three to six pages is sufficient) will skim off the emotional residue allowing you to set priorities and think more clearly. Try this practice for at least two or three months and you'll be amazed at how much you learn about yourself, your feelings, and the unconscious thoughts that bubble to the surface during the writing process.

If you are having a more severe problem managing your anger, keeping a formal anger diary will help you to monitor, log, and note the severity and frequency of the anger, and the feelings aroused by it. You can also record who and what situation provoked your anger. Several months of consistent diary entries will reveal certain patterns, responses, and behaviors, and will significantly help you control your anger.

Make Assertiveness Your Practice

Assertiveness, the hallmark of the brave woman, is the best defense against anger and is a learned behavior for many women. Firmly saying no, asking for help, setting limits, and communicating needs in both private and public settings are all ways of asserting yourself. Think about it: Do you ask a restaurant server if you can have more coffee or do say, "I would like some more coffee, please."

Many women need to practice assertiveness. Excellent targets for practicing self-assertion, particularly when angry, are the person who cuts in front of you in the grocery line, the car salesperson who tells you to come back with your husband "when you're serious," or the telemarketer who addresses you as "Marcia." Politely tell the person in line, "Excuse me, I was ahead of you." The car salesperson needs to know, "I make my own decisions about major purchases." "Have I met you before?" is the perfect response to the telemarketer's self-imposed familiarity.

Know When to Use Anger

In her best-selling book, *Women Who Run with the Wolves*, Clara Pinkola Estes (1992) writes: "There are times when it becomes imperative to release a rage that shakes the skies." In other words, sometimes you experience a deep betrayal or even a minor incident that is so outrageous, you feel compelled to respond in a display of inspired and powerful outrage.

Remember a time when you felt the need to detonate someone with your outrage. How did you handle it? Did you act on your emotions immediately or did you wait and respond in a self-empowered way?

If the person with whom you are upset is accessible, tell them that you need to talk to them. Your objective is to make them aware that their behavior has consequences, that the behavior may spell the demise of the relationship unless some amends can be made. For example, you might want to say: "I felt deeply hurt when you betrayed the trust of our relationship."

You may have an outrage toward a person who is not available or will never be accessible. In that case, write a letter to the individual describing exactly how you feel. Although you may choose to send them the letter, it is not always necessary. Often, just writing down your feelings will help you to feel better.

Ellen: A Brave New Path

Ellen waited three months, allowed her initial shock and anger to subside, and then confronted her friend Amy directly about a betrayal. Both belonged to a "breakfast club," a group of women going through divorces who convened over coffee on weekday mornings to share details of heir lives, swap divorce lawyer information, reveal their goals, and help each other strategize. Ellen didn't know that Amy was reporting back to and sleeping with Ellen's husband. Calling Amy took lots of mettle, but hearing her admit to her affair with Sam validated Ellen's outrage. Telling Amy directly how she felt allowed Ellen to release and articulate her anger.

Supercharge Your Bravery

Bold women who rechannel the anger they attach to negative experiences have a constant supply of motivation and fuel for achievement. By remembering a parent, a teacher, or a boss who expressed negativity and doubt in a healthy manner, you can use the memory to model your own behaviors.

The mechanism for supercharging your bravery is to prove that something isn't so. You negate and disprove the message of a hurt by doing the exact thing you were told you couldn't do. Your success and triumphs invalidate the oppression, pain, and hurt you experienced. The hurt was real, but you don't succumb to it, you disempower it.

Sandra: A Brave New Path

Sandra Bograd, now in her thirties, remembers her fury when a grade school teacher labeled her "retarded" because she tended to mumble in class. Bograd resolved to become "one of New Jersey's finest prosecuting attorneys" and a skilled communicator. Today she is a winning defense attorney.

Turn Anger Into Creativity and Humor

Any woman's anger can be turned into a short story or poem, stitched on a pillow, painted on a canvas, or translated into a stand-up comedy routine. Turning your anger into artwork or writing defuses its potency and allows you to right an injustice that's been perpetrated on you. It also allows you to speak to others who have experienced the same types of injustice. Visualizing or writing something provides an outlet for your anger and a way to work through it.

Playwrights, performance artists, comedians, novelists, and muralists routinely convert anger into art and rechannel their anger. Cathy, an improvisational actor from Chicago, says "kitchen harassment" during her day job as a waitress inspires her strong, angry characters, which then appear that night on stage. Clothing designer Eileen Fisher, angry at the way women's clothes are designed, created her own line and successfully markets clothes that fit and feel comfortable on real women's figures. The point is to couple your anger with your talents.

Live Well: The Best Revenge

The healthiest, most life-changing "revenges" transform the energy of anger into positive actions, acts of conviction, even long-held dreams. Is there some wrong that you want to right? Have you had an emotional shock that left you reeling and filled with anger? Visualization techniques can help fan the flames, redirect the anger, and focus the energy. The following exercise, adapted from *Female Rage: Unlocking Its Secrets, Claiming Its Power* (Valentis and Devane 1994), will help you reprogram your anger as an energy force.

Lie on your bed, count backwards from one hundred until you are relaxed and comfortable. Imagine you are standing in a pool house next to an empty swimming pool. Standing in the bottom of the pool is the person or the people who provoked your anger.

Recreate the scene that triggered your anger. Acknowledge the intensity of your feelings. Now turn on an imaginary faucet that produces a liquid that fills the pool and enters the eyes, ears, and mouths of your oppressors. As the liquid rushes over their heads, your anger recedes.

Next visualize the energy that produced your anger. See it in the form of a Bunsen burner emitting a powerful blue and gold flame. Feel the flame's power and warmth penetrate your body. Let it bathe and cover you like a comforting blanket. Each time you re-experience the anger, repeat this exercise.

Melissa: A Brave New Path

Melissa, the mother of two and a graduate student in women's studies and public policy, has dreamed, ever since her first pregnancy, of legalizing midwifery in New York State.

Turned off by traditional physicians whose approach clashed with hers on personal birthing choices and seemed "invasive and wrong-headed," Melissa started "listening to my insides for the first time" and decided, in her sixth month of pregnancy, not to give birth in the hospital.

"It was the most extraordinary thing I've ever done. Taking charge, taking control over my body and my baby, was incredibly empowering." Melissa birthed in a squatting position in the middle of a hexagonal pool. There were candles and incense burning and African music playing. Her baby was born underwater.

That birth has been the defining moment in Melissa's life. The decision has changed her attitudes and approach to others in every way. "You need anger to get courage. I was so angry at those doctors," she said. This event spurred Melissa toward the bravery needed to make midwifery legalization her life's mission.

Anger is the bedrock of bravery, the fuel that fires up your courage and supercharges your creativity. You have learned how to transform anger into energy and use it as a motivator to spur you on. The next chapter, the brave woman's guide to risk-taking, will show you how to take the bold risks that foster your sense of competency and self-esteem.

Chapter 9

Be a Bold Risk-Taker and Boundary Queen

Blaze Your Own Trails and Don't Let Others Trespass

Life is either a daring adventure or nothing.

—Helen Keller

To be brave you must take risks. Risk-taking is what separates the brave woman from her peers. You cannot grow and mature unless you risk. To risk is to let go of the known for the unknown, to reach for something better, more fulfilling, more meaningful, and not allow any fears of failure to stop you. You have no assurances when risking, but risking is essential for your personal growth and enhanced strength of character and maturity. You grow in wisdom and understanding when you take risks.

Dynamic strategy No. 10 is to become conversant with the process of self-assertive risk-taking and accepting the prospect of "failure." You can't take risks and succeed without failure. You'll learn that failure for the brave woman is a course correction, not an inherent part of her identity or a negative reflection of who she is as a person.

True Values and Beliefs: Your Bravery Compass

The brave new you, armed with your true values and beliefs, is a bold risk-taker:

- You risk falling in love and being rejected.

- You risk expressing your ideas and having them shot down.

- You have the courage of your convictions despite opposition.

- You doggedly pursue your destiny knowing that living bravely counts more than your final destination.

- You venture forth to fulfill your goals and dreams knowing, in advance, that not all your goals will be achieved, but many will, and that's all right.

Winfrey: A Brave New Path

Talk show host Oprah Winfrey is a bold risk-taker. She risked losing her high ratings when she decided to buck the trend toward trash television and instead produced a quality show that reflects her personal values and mission. That bold decision networked Oprah into the worlds of book and magazine publishing, academia, and psychology.

Based on Toni Morrison's literary masterpiece, *Beloved*, Oprah produced a film that was an artistic success but a commercial "flop," and she successfully defended her right of free speech in a court case instigated by Texas cattlemen who decried her on-air remarks about beef. She took a tremendous chance when she created a book club in a technological era. Oprah's Book Club has introduced millions of women and men to the pleasures of reading.

Oprah continues to take bold risks. Her magazine *O*, which pitches Oprah's positive attitude toward change and personal growth and encourages women to be brave, was itself a risky venture.

success comes down to her willingness to expose herself without the safety of her previous success. Oprah's risk-taking is multi-faceted and crosses diverse activities and challenges, including running a marathon, teaching a university-level seminar, acting, directing, and delivering a commencement address. Her risk-taking places Oprah in a constant state of becoming, someone who is always changing and growing, precisely because she continually is trying new things.

Honesty Must Be Your Policy

To risk is to be honest. This means peeling away false beliefs, unworkable commitments, senseless responsibilities, faithless friends, and destructive habits. You cannot grow and experience anything close to your potential without being absolutely honest with yourself and about your circumstances. To experience your bravery, you must act courageously to rid yourself of the emotional stumbling blocks holding you back and keeping you in secure but meaningless situations. You can no longer live a lie, you must change, you must risk. It's hard to give up the past and the familiarity of the present. But as a brave woman, it is the only choice you have.

To risk is to give up your false securities and the excuses you make about you and others. If you don't express your bravery by risking, you doubt yourself and your abilities. Without risking, you can never know how successful you could truly be in your work and personal life.

Many people look back on their lives with regret about their choices and long for a second chance to prove to themselves that they could do better. With hindsight there is no risk-taking, just the ability to look back and say, "if only." You see with unsettling clarity missed opportunities, squandered time and energy on the superficial and on empty activities, and you weep that you can't go back and do it differently—it's too late.

The brave woman knows that without aspirations her spirit and soul stagnate and lose vitality. To have a purpose is to be alive and to have energy. To thrust yourself wholeheartedly into your work, setbacks and all, is to make things happen. As a brave woman you won't settle for anything less—it is your birthright to become what you want to be, to create the life you want and to reap the rewards of the brave new you who dared to risk.

Dana Kennedy: Taking a Chance on Love

Dana Kennedy has taken chances all her life. The wife of Pulitzer Prize–winning novelist William Kennedy has been a bold risk-taker from the first time she put on a pair of ballet shoes. "I think of myself as confident," she says. "When you're confident, you can be fearless."

Dana was born in Puerto Rico and moved with her family to Spanish Harlem when she was a toddler. While her independent mother worked, Dana's grandmother, who lived to be 107, raised her favorite granddaughter to be strong and daring. Dana's first exposure to show business was ballet lessons supported by the Hetcher Foundation, which supplied the neighborhood children with ballet shoes and scholarships for dancing lessons. "You put your foot on a piece of paper and they drew an outline to measure the size of your slippers," she recalls. "From then on, I always had a dancer's mentality: the dedication, the oneness of mind. I bring the same kind of focus to everything I do. I jump into a challenge."

Her next challenge was auditioning for the New York High School of Performing Arts. Dancers from all the five boroughs were to perform the Mexican hat dance. Although she was trained in the style of the American Ballet Theatre, Dana convinced herself, "I have to do it, this is it!" She was accepted. "I must have projected confidence," she said. "I've found that talent is not as important as determination. Every audition I ever made was against all odds."

Her first professional audition was as a replacement for Shirley McLaine in the Broadway show *Me and Juliet*. Dana's girlfriend counseled her to wear a red scarf. "The scene was right out of *All that Jazz*, or *A Chorus Line*," she remembers. "Hundreds of expectant girls with legs way up to there, and triple fake eyelashes. Each one of us had to sing "Blue Skies." I was in awe and dumbstruck. This was the most courageous thing I ever did. I was still there in the round of fifty, then ten, and then it came down to me and two other dancers. Richard Rodgers was sitting there and gestured to his assistant after we did our number. 'The one in the red scarf,' he said. My name was Anna Daisy, and when they asked me for a stage name, I said Dana." Dana went on to appear in *Pajama Game*, *New Faces of 1956*, and *The Pleasure Dome*.

That Christmas she went home to Puerto Rico with Maggie Smith. Two days later she met a young journalist. He asked her out for New Year's Eve, but she turned him down because she wanted to keep up the family tradition of all being together at midnight. "He looked so heartbroken, I told him I would go out after the family gathering." She didn't know it but the second chapter of her life had just begun.

Bill wrote to her in New York: "Dear Jelly Bean Love: I'm a writer, I am not well-known, but the world is my oyster." "I had tremendous confidence in Bill. I took the risk and married him ten dates later. I knew that long-distance relationships don't work. I gave up show business. I had accomplished what I wanted to do, and relationships were more important to me. I have smart instincts. I'm always ready for a new adventure, a new phase." Dana's grand jet into marriage was "with my heart and soul."

Dana and Bill moved to Albany, New York, Bill's hometown and the literary landscape familiar from his seven novels. Dana raised their family, learned new skills, and supported Bill's aspirations, all the while maintaining her own spirit and identity. She opened a combination dance studio and retail clothing store to help support the family during the leaner years, and her students have performed with the New York City Ballet.

She has shared and delighted in Bill's great successes and remains his partner, confidante, best critic, and fellow adventurer. Dana's fearlessness and boldness is reflected in every aspect of their life together. "I like being ready for what comes next," she said. A look inside her handbag proves her statement true: there's a pepper mill, a sewing kit, the ubiquitous cell phone, a Swiss knife, a spoon, and a flashlight. Being prepared for adventure certainly helps with bold risk-taking.

The Process of Risk

As a brave woman you know that risking means that in the process of gaining something greater for your life, you will lose something. As you take risks, loss comes when your plans don't work out as expected. You may go back to school and realize that it isn't right for you. You may start a new business venture or profession only to be disappointed that it was not all that you projected it would be. A new lover may disappoint you, or an established relationship may fail. This is why risks are challenging—there are no guarantees and the potential for setbacks and failure is always there.

To be brave enough to risk puts you face-to-face with your fears and anxiety, with potential loss. Not risking means you never test your fears or push through your anxieties. This allows your fears to run your life and limit your choices. Happiness and fulfillment then elude you, the world in your eyes becomes too dangerous for risk-taking.

To risk and succeed, however, is to outgrow your fears, to gain confidence, and to experience more courage for bigger and better things. If you only seek security in your life and avoid identifying your true feelings about situations and yourself, you'll find yourself imprisoned in a straitjacket with little breathing space or maneuverability. If you think that your circumstances will change for the better without doing something about them, you're fooling yourself. Letting events shape your life will only make situations worse, not better. You must take action to feel alive, to feel worthy; nothing less will do.

Four Risk-Taking Steps toward Bravery

Risk-taking is simultaneously art, logic, and a dynamic process. It involves self-questioning, tapping into your emotions, learning to let go, and taking action. The four risk-taking steps toward bravery and the exercises that follow are a blueprint for dealing with any risk, large or small.

Step One: Identify What You Want

To risk and be brave requires that you know what you're after. You must have goals that inflame your passions, that speak to you deeply and meaningfully, and that once fulfilled will make you stronger, wiser, more authentic, and mature.

Remember accomplishing your goals requires the commitment to what is genuinely important to you. It is counterproductive to strive for goals based on others' expectations of you, or because others believe they know what is right for you. You must aim your sights on what truly speaks to *you*; anything less and your successes ultimately will be disappointments, and will hold little long-term joy or meaning.

The Illusion of Security

If you do not identify yourself as a risk-taker and you cling to security, you should recognize that even in achieving "security" you've taken some risk. As author Erica Jong (1964) says, "If you don't risk anything, you risk even more." Accepting circumstances that seem to fall in your lap, or allowing events and people to decide what is acceptable for you, following a prescribed way of doing things because of tradition or because "that's the way things are done," still requires some risk, albeit it's mostly stifling.

Everything in your life is impermanent, nothing is forever. The risk in this situation is to live within the illusion that if you hold on to things and situations you will be "secure." The brave woman knows this is an illusion: What you gain through the need for security can just as easily be lost as what you gain through risk-taking. To be brave is to know that lasting security comes only by utilizing the strength, courage, and inner security that you create for yourself. Fear is a constant companion in your risk-taking, though it doesn't have to stop you. Fear, at its best, can help propel you forward.

Fulfilling Your Desires

To have reached this point in your life means you have taken some risks, and without further risking, you will not get to where you want to be. The journey of the brave risk-taker starts with desires that need to be fulfilled. Ask yourself the following questions:

- Do I need to feel better about myself?

- Do I want to know myself better?

- Do I want better relationships?

- Do I want work that is better and more challenging?

- Do I want to make more money?

- Do I feel stuck?

- Does life hold little excitement for me?

- Do I long for something better?

- Do I want to wake up to life's possibilities?

To be a brave risk-taker requires a plan with certain rules to follow. Start with identifying your feelings. Did you truthfully answer the questions above? Your feelings communicate everything about your current state of affairs: what you should accept or reject, what you should hold on to or discard, and when it's time to move on. Your feelings are the barometer that measures the quality and meaningfulness of your life. Learn to listen to them closely and never run away from them.

Step Two: Learn the Language of Emotion

To be brave is to learn the "language" of your feelings. To be brave is to feel what's inside of you. Anything less is to stifle your growth and sabotage your efforts. Feelings and emotions are volatile, and they are as varied as the many situations that you encounter during a given day.

You can count on your emotions to:

- Linger and override situations.

- Help you to listen and trust the whisperings of your own inner voice.

- Signal that you have to start to do things differently and create a different landscape for your life.

Emotions linger. They are disquieting and never seem to go away. They nudge us to take notice. Emotions are the messengers of change that tell us that it's now time to flex the muscles of our courage—don't ignore them.

Rid Yourself of Emotional Buildup

To be brave is to risk loosening your defenses and to be more open to yourself and your feelings. A defense is an unconscious mechanism you deploy to block, displace, or express feelings with which you find it hard to deal. You develop defenses to protect yourself from criticism and to preserve your sense of well-being. The stronger your defenses, the more numb you become and the less you are able to experience pleasure or pain.

To grow, change, and create a new life for yourself requires you to feel pain, sorrow, and loss, and not to run away. What you feel motivates you to change your life and to start living more authentically.

Building a Fortress of Defenses

Being direct with your feelings and not hiding or denying them means that you don't store them up or ignore them. In many instances, however, you may unconsciously be operating from behind a fortress of defenses that contribute to your controlling your feelings. When you express yourself based on your defenses, you are the least authentic and real. For example, you may:

- *Overintellectualize* your feelings and remove yourself from the emotions of your experiences by becoming very clinical and "emotionally robotic."

- *Minimize* or *trivialize* a situation and its impact on you.

- *Pull a reversal* and act in the opposite manner to someone or a situation than you really feel. For instance, if you're furious, you act extra sweet, or you act as if you like a person when you really despise them.

- *Pretend* that certain situations or people are not important to you when, in fact, the opposite is true.

- Act like *"you're above it all,"* not bothering to waste your time on matters of little concern when, truthfully, the issue in question is very important to you.

Putting up your defenses is a very exhausting proposition: To "protect" yourself from your own emotions requires energy. You begin to displace stored up emotions inappropriately on the wrong people or situations. When you do take some risks you then may feel angry, or depressed, or anxious or even guilty; even though you may be doing what's best for you, it simply doesn't feel right. This emotional burden causes many people to stop in their tracks unable to change or grow. They become stagnant and miserable with their situation and with themselves.

When you admit your true feelings, your defenses begin to fall away.

When you're afraid and tend to deny your fear, ask yourself the following questions:

- What are you afraid of happening or losing?

- What's the worst that could happen?

- If the worst happens, what are the steps you could take to make things right again?

- How can you ensure that the worst doesn't happen?

When you're hurt and you pretend someone didn't get to you, ask yourself the following questions:

- Who hurt you?

- Why did the situation happen?

- Could you have stopped that individual from doing what she/he did?

- Did you make your feelings known at the time?

When you're angry at someone and are acting sweet to that same person, ask yourself the following questions:

- Why are you angry?

- Were you disappointed?

- Were you used or being taken advantage of?

- Were you insulted or made fun of?

The brave woman knows that she must be open and sensitive to what she feels. To accept your emotions, whether they are exhilarating or uncomfortable, is to allow your creativity to flow and to have the energy to express it. Fuel from your emotions ignites your bravery and propels you forward. You then accomplish your goals and have a life of joy, brimming with creative expression that many only experience in their dreams.

Climb Every Mountain, Step by Step

As a brave woman, see yourself as a mountain climber. Your goal is to reach the summit where the view is beautiful and reserved only for the few who risk the climb. Most people look at the top of the majestic mountaintop from ground level, vowing that when conditions are right they'll make the climb. Others don't even think about it because they feel they don't have the talent or natural ability or the equipment to make the climb. They give up before they even start.

The brave woman knows that to reach that mountaintop, she has to make her climb one step at a time. This approach or psychological mindset dissolves her fears and reservations. With each successful step her confidence and bravery increase; she knows she can do it. She faces impasses on her climb and sees these as challenges to overcome. She gains confidence in her problem-solving ability that feeds her courage and determination to reach the top. She will not be denied the experience and the exhilaration of reaching the heights and seeing the view.

Step Three: Take the Plunge and Create a Plan

The third step in risk-taking is to create a plan, a roadmap with incremental steps leading to your goal achievement. Your dreams—what you want to accomplish—may seem overwhelming at first and difficult to reach. Creating a step-by-step process in reaching the "impossible" is to psychologically make your progress more manageable, buoying up your courage to persist and persevere.

1. **In your journal, label or give your risk a title.** For example: "A Step-by-Step Plan for Publishing My First Poem."

2. **Identify all the steps required**. In the case of the poem, that may include selecting, polishing, and revising one of your best poems. You will want to get some feedback on your

piece by attending a workshop, consulting a teacher or a mentor. You will need to buy and consult some writer's journals, a magazine, or check the Internet for the best outlet for publishing your particular kind of poem.

3. **Arrange and prioritize the steps you listed in No. 2**. What are you going to do first? Make a timetable. Write down an actual "drop dead" date when you will lick the stamp and send your work out into the publishing universe. Each time you complete a step, check it off.

4. **Constantly revise your plan**. Make adjustments for delays, obstacles, and unforeseen interruptions. Choose one day a week to review and adjust your plan.

To be a brave risk-taker means stepping out from the familiar into a world not clearly defined—not into a minefield, but into a rich, leafy forest, filled with enchanting surprises and some pitfalls. It requires preparation that is not foolproof, but allows you to deal with the hazards of the journey more effectively, providing you greater confidence to persevere and not give up. You must have some understanding of the uncharted waters that you're traversing to navigate successfully.

Be Deliberate, Not Impulsive

Never confuse deliberate risk-taking with impulsive behavior. Impulsive risk-taking doesn't come from your bravery and your sense of purpose, it comes from needing to prove oneself, the need to win no matter what, the need to beat the competition, exact revenge, or the unconscious need to actually sabotage yourself and fail.

Each step you take should have a reasonable time frame for completion. Each step completed toward your goal gains you confidence and fuels your determination and desire. Always make room for the unforeseen, for delays, mistakes, and detours along the way. You must have flexibility with your plans so that they coincide with the inevitable surprises that you encounter. Plan for problems and devise strategies on how to handle them. Keep in mind, too, it's impossible to plan for all unforeseen challenges.

Success, Confidence, and Bravery

With your increasing success you become more confident. As your confidence mounts, your bravery strengthens and is fueled by your successful experiences. The adage, "Nothing breeds success like success," is certainly true of the brave woman. You develop a success-oriented motivation that is so strong, the setbacks along the way are merely inconveniences or even rest stops for revising your plans—your setbacks and failures do not become calamities, they are learning experiences along your journey to successful completion of your goals.

As you build "emotional muscle" with your risking, your future risks become bolder and more exhilarating as you raise the stakes to higher levels. Your bravery becomes boundless and stronger.

Expect and Accept Fears to Arise

Understand that as a brave risk-taker, you will experience fear and doubts as you forge ahead. Expect it and accept it, but don't let it stop you. You will also experience aliveness, that energy-filled sense of excited anticipation because you're doing something new, something challenging. Your journey releases your "growth hormones," your bravery and confidence. The release of your positive feelings reinforces the need and the desire to continue to completion that which you've started.

Barbara: A Brave New Path

Barbara found her dream job working with food and wine at a winery and restaurant complex in Carmel Valley. For her first twenty-eight years, she didn't know that she is a person who thrives on change and working through a challenge. She lived alone in an apartment on the south side of town, close to her parents, in a close-knit, comfortable community in upstate New York. She had a short commute to the public utility company where she worked and where she met Dave.

The most courageous move Barbara ever made was to leave her hometown and move to Florida with Dave. She also decided (against her parents' wishes) not to get married but to live with Dave away from her friends and family. Barbara and Dave had one-year renewable contracts. For four years, they "gave each other another year," and then got married once they moved to California.

Barbara said: "I'm a great one for T-charts. If you need to take a risk or make a decision about something, you divide a piece of paper in half and add up the pluses and minuses." Barbara's system has worked through all kinds of job decisions and career moves. She always knows when it is the right time to leave a position and move on to the next challenge.

When they moved to California's Silicon Valley, Barbara worked for six years in a motivating and challenging environment. "Chaos and challenge make me light up," Barbara said. "I like to see how I can put the pieces together to figure things out."

Barbara decided to leave her job because she wanted to work in a more technologically savvy environment. "I made a list of what I wanted—voice mail, e-mail, PC rather than a Mac system—and took a risk by taking a job in an insurance company. I hated it, but at least I knew that I didn't want that." After two more tries, Barbara found the winery. "Things have a way of working out, if you do take the risks," she said. "The point is that life is full of choices. I can't imagine what would have happened if I hadn't taken chances."

The Do's and Don'ts of Risk-Taking

As a brave risk-taking woman, you face the unique challenges of your gender. Although our society is changing and allows women the freedom of expression that was, until recently, limited or nonexistent, prescribed gender roles are still strong enough to cause you doubt about what you should be doing.

You may be criticized for getting ahead, for doing what's right for you. You may be told to stop trying to be like a man and learn to accept what you have. You may also be told how ungrateful and unappreciative you've become because you want to change things that you should accept don't need changing. The pressures can be severe. But as a brave woman you listen to your conscience, your feelings, and your inner voice that tells you you must change, you must move on. It's your life and no one can live it for you.

As a brave woman, don't confuse people's opinions as facts. Listen to others selectively and use wise counsel to better yourself. Discard the opinions of people who want to hold you back and keep you where you are. Surround yourself with successful people, who understand your plans and dreams, and who support your endeavors.

As a brave woman you know that successful people support the success of others, they are the brave woman's guides and mentors. Don't try to grow your garden in a weed patch. The weeds will overwhelm the fresh budding of the flower that you've just planted. Don't talk to people about your plans and dreams, particularly with people who are threatened by your success, who envy your bravery, who secretly wish that you would fail.

When you talk to people who are unhappy with their own lives, and you tell them what you're doing, it throws into question why they are not doing something about their own lives. Your changes upset and threaten them. They're not ready to risk and change, so they put down you and your plans or they tell you it can't be done. Listen to the successful people who've walked the same road you're now traveling: they will tell you that it can and should be done. Plant your garden in this rich soil and watch it bloom and prosper.

Step Four: Take Action

Now, with plans in place it's time to commit to action. As a brave woman you know that no matter what you anticipate, the true reality of what you're doing hits you with unexpected force. It's one thing to think about what will happen, it's another thing to experience it. The feelings you stir up in others and the feelings that you stir up in yourself may cause you to doubt the wisdom of what you are doing. This is a period of vulnerability where your fears and doubts reassert themselves and people's reactions of dismay and anger may cause you to feel guilty and badly.

You may fear being rejected, losing others' love, or being alone. But as a brave woman you remain undaunted and unstoppable. You will not be denied your future or your new life. Understand that when your family, friends, or colleagues react negatively to what you're doing, or they don't understand what's gotten into you, or things don't compute from their perspective, they're reacting to change, too.

What they don't understand about you and what you're doing, they fear and criticize. They want the old person back. As a brave risk-taker you know that once you've made the commitment to change things and put your plan into action, there's no turning back. You've already parachuted out of the plane. You're committed to your course.

Chapter 10

Live On Your Terms

Be More Authentic and Assertive in Relationships

*For most of us, today more than ever, love is the
primary mode of risk-taking, of the venture
without which there can be no sense of self-realization.*

—Ethel S. Person

You will now crack open the next babushka doll. She represents you in the kingdom of relationships. You have allowed your bravery to surface. You know how to take risks. You have the courage to surmount obstacles. And you have the incentive to create a new vision and direction for your life. Now it's time to embark upon the path toward bravery in your closest relationships. Personal relationships are the most important yet challenging aspects of our lives, and they require courage, honesty, and authenticity to keep them healthy. When they are honest, compelling, and mutually respectful, relationships thrive. Hide the truth, bury the issues and conflicts, and relationships grow cold and die.

In dynamic strategy No. 10, you will use your bravery to form a strong and more authentic bond with your partner and eliminate inequalities in your relationships. You will acquire the tools for manifesting your courage to be your own person and to be more straightforward and honest with people.

Knowing that your opinions, thoughts, and perceptions really do count, you will apply your bravery to relationships. Learning to be direct will give you a greater sense of self-possession and imbue your relationships with meaning. You will gain a greater sense of self-respect and inner power as a woman.

You will be capable of withstanding the pressures of living in a consumerist culture that emphasizes air-brushed images over substance, expediency over doing what you know is right, and throwaway love over the hard work and rewards of creating committed, mutually rewarding relationships.

In the last section of this chapter, you will be inspired by other brave women and encouraged to develop muses and mentor relationships.

Relationship Decisions: Choose Character over Charm

When choosing a college, making a decision about a job, deciding where to live, even writing a paper, you probably take time to do research, investigate many angles, think things through, add up the pluses and minuses, and then make an informed decision. Love is different, you tell yourself. It's chemistry. You'll ruin it if you make romantic choices based on logic or calculation; all the spontaneity and romance goes out of it.

Remember, the initial passion and rush of a relationship last two years at the most. The hard part comes when those chemicals lose potency and you need to work to make love last. And love is dangerous. There are deep, irrational strains in love. Relationships change all the time.

The brave choice in love is an informed one. Check out your lover and check out how you feel. What does your gut tell you? Have you looked beyond the surface charm? Choose your partner as you would choose a college, a job, even a stock. Research the "company's" history, read between the lines of a glossy marketing report, check out the performance, growth potential. Is there congruency between what your lover does and says? What are the company's values? Do they support tobacco? Do they enhance and preserve beauty and the environment?

If you are single, make a list of the qualities you want in a partner or a friend. What tops your list? If you have a life partner, compare him or her against the list of qualities you want in a partner. Have you made the right choice?

Mary and John: A Brave New Path

As coauthors and life partners, Mary and John have been walking a brave new path together for more than ten years. John's "relationship vision" is a model he calls *interdependency*, a connection based on mutual respect and support that comes together when necessary and provides for each partner's independence and forays into the world. His bottom lines for a relationship are total honesty, no jealousy, and the mutual airing of issues and problems as they crop up. Debate, contention, and discussion are integral to an alive and ongoing relationship.

John's model was totally foreign to Mary, who had allowed herself to be completely dominated in her first marriage and whose family members had competed with one another even over food morsels. Issues and conflicts were never aired and discussed, but turned into illnesses and the domestic equivalent of nuclear war. Mary had to learn how to defend herself, how to discuss mutual concerns, and how to work through issues and problems.

Often, Mary is asked, "Isn't it difficult being married to a psychotherapist?" Her answer is, "Yes and no." John is Mary's husband and partner, not her therapist.

When they were first married (it's the second marriage for both of them), they had to contend with personality, family, and turf adjustments, and they discussed at length their personal ideas about relationships. John made it clear that he would leave his therapy work behind at the office, but that he viewed their relationship as a route toward self-actualization and positive transformation. He wasn't kidding. John is trained to help people positively change their lives, and he works on himself all the time. John and Mary both have changed drastically during the years they've been together, and they believe it's for the better. They've successfully adjusted—and continue to readjust—to each other's quirks, strengths, weaknesses, thought patterns, and communication and work styles. The greatest journey, the most intense drama ever experienced, is to work though the process of loving someone.

Conscious Decisions toward Brave Relations

It takes bravery to live with a partner and to live without one. Ask yourself the following questions to gain insight into how you think and feel about significant relationships, the degree of honesty you bring to them, your sense of autonomy, and your choices:

1. Would you rather live with a partner who tells you how to think, how to be, and what to do, or with someone who calls on you to be strong and committed to your beliefs and principles, and to assert your independence?

2. Would you rather be alone than with someone who is threatened by your growth and changes, and who holds you back? One brave woman said, "The bravest thing I ever did was to leave someone I loved, because I knew he wasn't right for me. Now I'm alone and it's hard, but it was better than living a lie and raising false expectations in my partner."

3. Are you able to be open and honest with your partner? Can you agree to disagree on some issue and accept the other's point of view as valid too?

4. Do you see your relationship as a creative, mutual growth process?

5. Are you comfortable living on your own? Women who feel that something is missing or that they are not complete without a man discover that another person will not solve their problems or make them complete. You are already complete in yourself.

The information you glean from answering the questions above lets you gauge the role bravery plays in you relationships. Hopefully, you have discovered that you're involved in a creative, mutually supportive relationship where there is open exchange and encouragement for one another. Perhaps you're content living on your own or have recently made the decision to break off with someone who wasn't the right person for you.

If you honestly assess, however, that you're with someone who inhibits your growth, or that your partner tells you how you should think, look, and act, you might want to write more extensively about the issues you've identified. After reviewing the pluses and minuses of the relationship, consider talking with a professional about how you can change your attitudes and behavior. Remember *you* are the only one who allows someone else to dictate how you should be.

Scrambled versus Fried Eggs

How eggs are prepared provide an apt metaphor for the nature of friendships and relationships. Think of yourself and your partner or you and your friend as a pair of uncooked eggs. Now "cook" them together in your mind. Are you a pair of scrambled or fried eggs? Are you and your partner fused? In other words, are you totally whisked up into one mixture (relationship) or are you mutually interdependent?

In the case of the finished scrambled eggs in the pan, the original eggs have disappeared and the result is a fluffy bright yellow mixture. This combination leads to a different texture and taste, to be sure, but the original "eggs" have disappeared. A fused relationship is like scrambled eggs. Someone loses his/her identity, and it's usually the woman.

The fried eggs present a different picture. There are still two distinctive egg yolks surrounded and mutually joined by the whites. You can distinguish one egg from the other, but you can also see them as part of a whole. Fried eggs are the interdependent love match between equals. Each partner has kept their identity in tact and, at the same time, they participate in the bond.

The fried eggs embody the paradox and tensions inherent in being a woman in relationship: you are one, and also two at once (Leonard 1998). The challenge for the brave woman is to preserve her identity and be herself in her relationships. Never sacrifice or give up a part of yourself just to keep a relationship afloat. Suppressing who you are and what you really want to say only breeds resentment and comes out through unhealthy outlets and passageways.

A Recipe for Successful Partnering

Being yourself in a relationship means taking the risk to be emotionally "naked" or vulnerable with your partner. True intimacy is created with the following ten ingredients of the brave woman's recipe for successful partnering:

1. As a brave woman you are completely honest in your relationship with your partner, and they are completely honest with you. Honesty doesn't mean being brutally honest in a way that hurts your partner, but *tactfully honest* as a way of drawing out your partner, so that they feel safe enough to talk with you and to help ameliorate problems and impasses in the relationship.

2. In the brave woman's relationship you are comfortable and vulnerable with your partner. Trust and respect for each other allows for this.

3. As a brave woman you are free to be yourself with your partner, there are no pretenses, no play-acting, there is just you.

4. As a brave woman you know that you don't have to "adjust" to your partner when alone with them. Whenever you feel that you can't be yourself with your partner, know you are leaving a part of you out of the relationship to make it work, making it less real, less honest, less vibrant, less alive.

5. As a brave woman you are not lonely in your relationship because when you are relating to your partner you're completely there, heart and soul.

6. As a brave woman you don't sacrifice who you are for the sake of the relationship. Retain your power and your relationship remains strong.

7. As a brave woman your relationship is built on the mutual self-respect of two equals who share the joys and burdens of life together. Each of you is encouraged to become who and what you want to be.

8. As a brave woman you know that your relationship is a dynamic system of growth and change that is mutually supported.

9. As a brave woman you love your partner as they are. You don't need to mold and shape them to your needs. This allows them to love you more.

10. As a brave woman you don't possess or own your partner. They are free to be independent and to be themselves.

Every Relationship Has a Contract

Some relationships have liberal views while others relationships are bound by traditional roles. Many times these expectations are never discussed. The result is an unwritten contract—unspoken expectations you bring into a relationship or marriage—which results in you being emotionally disappointed and misunderstood. Your partner may not be relating to you as you think they should within the context of your relationship. Meanwhile, your partner hasn't a clue about your unspoken expectations.

There are expectations and unwritten contracts in almost all relationships. Based on your background, you have a vision of how relationships and your partner should be. Write a few sentences that describe your vision of a perfect relationship. Now have your partner write down his/her vision. Compare them. Are they the same or different? The shock may come when you discover your partner doesn't necessarily share the same views, values, or responsibilities of a relationship.

Leandra: A Brave New Path

No one thought she had the courage, the nerve, or the lingerie.

—Film description of
Shirley Valentine

First a Broadway show and then a film, *Shirley Valentine* (Russell 1989) is the story of a bored suburban housewife living in England who chances an adventure on a Greek island when a friend invites her on a vacation. The friend ends up not going, but Shirley spends the summer away from her husband learning to live on her own terms, recapturing her youthful personality, and living her dream.

Leandra is a real life Shirley Valentine. Married for twenty-eight years, Leandra is the director of a language center in northern California. She explained: "I have a totally supportive, loving husband who is my best friend and publicity agent." Three years ago, Leandra needed a "Shirley Valentine" summer abroad. She remembers sitting on the plane to Italy wondering, "What am I doing?" Then, eight weeks later, she wondered why she had never before spent a summer on her own. She made all the travel and lodging arrangements on her own, staying in an apartment in one of Rome's most ancient and mystical settings, dining with friends, touring the countryside, and communicating regularly via the Internet with her husband.

"I loved being on my own for that period, and I loved returning to California. When I got off the plane after two months, my husband was yelling "Buon' giorno!" in the crowd at the airport. He was wearing a gondolier's hat and carrying a huge loaf of garlic bread."

The experience was a risk that strengthened their marriage and Leandra's self-confidence. She has two children, a daughter in her twenties who teaches at a college in Texas, and a mildly autistic, high-functioning, developmentally disabled son who lives in his own condominium where friends and family visit.

"I have always been very protective of my son," said Leandra, "and have never wanted him away from me. It was an extremely difficult choice when I agreed to put him in a special boarding school for developmentally disabled adolescents. I was so tempted to bring him home after weekend visits, but I resisted—it was really difficult, but the decision to take him out of a regular high school made a huge difference. It was one of my bravest moments."

The Bearer of Good and Bad News

The staying power of your intimate relationships is directly related or proportional to how honest you are willing to be—if you're not afraid to tell the bad news as well as the good news. Many people shy away from truth-telling in their relationships, they cover up their real thoughts and mask their needs to sustain what they think is their "likeability."

Catherine, a forty-four-year-old professional gardener, says, "I am instinctively brave and honest, and these traits cost me popularity. I can't play the game that girls play. I only say things when I mean them, and I don't like insincerity. I have a core of good friends, but I've found that men, more than women, tend to be straightforward and blunt. They have less need to be liked."

An overarching need to be liked, or concerns about personal popularity or about others' opinions, deprive many people of the joys of vital and ongoing relationships. Friendships and romantic partnerships require openness and honesty for longevity. Don't hold back your opinions. Be frank and honest with the people in your life, but tell the truth tactfully. Make it clear when people do or say something that goes against your grain. Speak up if you're feeling manipulated or drawn into a situation with which you're not comfortable. Remember, everyone has flaws. Never resort to humiliation, but protect your values and boundaries.

Clashing Values Challenge Your Bravery

Many times being brave means doing what you believe is right even when it's not expedient or the easiest thing for you to do. The

American culture prizes expediency—the "you snooze you lose" idea or "what's in it for me" attitudes are commonplace and more condoned than they were in previous decades. People fear taking the ethical high ground for many reasons, and sometimes, values and ethics seem old-fashioned.

Kathleen, for instance, was raised with what she calls "old world" values. "I can't lie," she says. "I have to tell the truth. My favorite literary character is Cordelia from Shakespeare's *King Lear*. In the play, Cordelia doesn't feed her father's ego with false words, still she's there when he really needs her, even though he's banished her from his kingdom. That's brave. My children think I'm very strict. I find it hard to form close relationships because of my tendency to be blunt, but that's the way I run my life."

Clashing values between generations are particularly challenging. When dealing with children, you compete with peers' values, the impact of culture, and other adults' value systems. Be clear and remain true to your own values. Remind children—and even other adults—that mistakes are inevitable and part of the learning process. Each day you have the opportunity to reinvent yourself.

Competing values are especially challenging in life partnerships. Your ethnic and religious backgrounds, your ideas and values about money, and your political views may diverge from your partner's. Recognize that a clash of values' reveals that there is a difference in values—it doesn't mean that one's bad or good. Discuss your differences and your feelings about those differences. Understand that there are certain values and beliefs your partner holds that he/she cannot change. Learn to live with those differences and not be threatened by them.

The strongest relationships are those in which two people allow and encourage their partners to grow and change personally and professionally, which means that values and priorities are shifting. For instance, what was once unimportant now may be in the foreground. Understand that unless relationships are dynamic and changing, they're stagnant and empty.

Be Brave with Your Vulnerabilities

Many people fear being open and vulnerable in their relationship. They fear being hurt, or rejected and criticized by the person most important in their lives. Because of these fears, they shut down, clam up, hide under the bed covers, or sit in front of the television or computer and stop talking. The irony is that these "solutions" contribute even more to the relationship's demise. Some have tried being more open and honest only to be taken advantage of by their "insensitive" partners. They vow never to let their guard down again. They withdraw and try to keep the peace at the expense of honesty and truthfulness. As both partners become less involved with each other to keep the relationship bearable, the very thing they do to keep the peace in the relationship is the very thing that further damages it.

There are many reasons why relationships go wrong. Ultimately, having a fighting chance for any relationship requires the courage to be totally honest with your partner. The brave woman always strives for this and expects her partner to do the same, anything less and the relationship begins to suffer. When you fear openness and vulnerability, the result is miscommunication and the pain and resentment that arise from it.

To be a brave woman is to be authentic, honest, and straightforward in your relationship. Most couples find this approach a difficult and daunting task. Many relationships that held promise and happiness at the beginning begin to languish because one or both partners stop communicating honestly. Their wishes, thoughts, expectations and feelings become a private affair.

As secrets in a relationship build up, love diminishes then disappears; real and imagined slights and hurts are never talked about. Instead one or both partners hold in their grudges and resentments. Their feelings build up like steam in a pressure cooker. A seemingly insignificant incident causes an explosion of intense emotions. There are hurt feelings all around. The partner who "overreacted" feels guilt. The person experiencing the attack is angry, hurt, and resentful. It doesn't always end there as partners duel back and forth in a battle of wills and self-righteousness.

In some relationships couples stop any meaningful communicating altogether, preferring to keep things at a very superficial and "civil" level. People in this type of relationship go through the motions with their spouses just to get through the day—love and caring for each other long gone.

Be Brave in Your Relationships

The list that follows includes attitudes and risks for being closer to your partner, sharing your innermost self, and keeping your relationship alive and vital. As you read through each point, think of its opposite. For instance, do you pretend situations are okay when they're not, or do you believe that feelings of love or indifference are fixed and don't change every day, even every few hours depending on what you are feeling and what happens to you?

To be brave in your relationship is to:

- Be honest, open, committed, thoughtful, giving, accepting, loyal, vulnerable resilient, flexible, and expressive.
- Respect your partner's differences.
- Honor and acknowledge the uniqueness of your partner.
- Share your thoughts and feelings.
- Promote freedom for both partners.
- Support each other's growth.
- Compromise: Do not mold or shape your partner to your self-created specifications.
- Not think your partner can make up for what you lack in yourself.
- Create a relationship between two equals.
- Not control someone.
- Not be competitive.
- Not be completely dependent.
- Respect your partner's sensitivities.
- Not sacrifice a part of yourself to make a relationship function.
- Be interdependent—not to be dependent or aloof and distant.
- Act from freedom of choice, not habit or coercion.
- Know that your partner's feelings are important.
- Love yourself, have a relationship with yourself, then share it with your partner.
- Risk rejection, criticism, and hurt, and talk about your own hurt and pain.
- Not pretend things are okay when they aren't.
- Not deny, ignore, or minimize problems and issues.
- Face conflict—don't avoid it.
- Eliminate all jealousy.
- Understand your feelings change from day-to-day.
- Not have unspoken expectations and unexpressed feelings toward your partner.

Bravery is an essential if not crucial element in intimate relationships. It takes courage to chance intimacy, to risk experiencing the pain and pleasures of love and its loss, and to be vulnerable with your partner.

Be Inspired by Other Brave Women

The heroines you embrace, your musings, and your daydreams reveal much about what makes you tick, what's important to you, and what you wish to become and accomplish. Their biographies dare you to pursue your life's possibilities, give us glimpses into your dreams and future lives, and ignite you with renewed energy. Who are your heroines? From what role models do you draw strength: a parent, a favorite aunt, an ancestor, a teacher, a mythic heroine, or a well-known public figure?

Dynamic strategy No. 10 includes identifying your inspirational muses and mentors, then absorbing and learning from them. These brave women and men instruct you on your path, and their example can rouse in you a helpful, inspiring "if she can do it, I can do it" attitude.

Finding Mentors, Role Models, and Muses

To achieve your indomitable spirit and bravery, to chart the most meaningful course for your life requires role models, muses, and mentors. Mentors serve as teachers and role models, gurus and allies who take a personal interest in your professional life and personal growth. They help nourish your talents and abilities in your quest for achievement. Often they enter your life just when you need them or when you are ready for the mental, emotional, creative, or intellectual growth spurts they facilitate. They are teachers, role models, coaches, and cheerleaders all rolled into one. Having a mentor and being a mentor are equally rewarding experiences.

Mentor-apprenticeship relationships have a long and distinguished history. In ancient Greece, the mentor-protégée relationship, most often between a young and older man, was prized more highly than a heterosexual marriage. Some mentors are literal teachers, while others show up in our lives mysteriously, when the timing's right. A mentor/role model can appear in a formalized relationship as a therapist, a rabbi, a minister, a priest, or a coach, or more casually as a neighbor, someone we read about, or a client.

Mentors can be parental or older sibling figures—surrogate mothers, fathers, brothers, sisters. Mentors are sometimes soul mates or the attachment may turn into a romantic involvement. Think of the great painter Georgia O'Keefe and her mentor and lover Alfred Steiglitz, or the celebrated love between poets Elizabeth Barrett and Robert Browning. These pairs' artistic productions and love lives were inextricably intertwined.

Inspire Your Inner Muses

Mentors can inspire you from the inside—you can use them to urge your inner muses, imagining your mentors in your mind's eye and ears as you write, perform, compose music, give a speech, or negotiate a problem or a deal.

Mentors in the professional sphere may lead you to unforeseen opportunities. They may crack the glass ceiling you bump up against, or generally help to pave the way for your successes. This feature of mentoring is particularly helpful for women who need an extra edge to gain entry into various networks, whether they are of the "good old boys" or the "good old girls" variety.

Admiration from Afar

You may admire your role model from a distance. Nicki views Nelson Mandela as her ideal mentor. The image of the South African national hero, who fought and went to prison to protest apartheid and the segregation of blacks and whites, resonates in her mind at times when she requires strength. "He's so strong, really strong. He spent twenty years in prison for a great cause. He came out whole and a leader. Now that's being brave."

You may go on a quest in search of your gurus or find them next door. You may want to study with a well-known potter, apprentice with a high-powered agent, take classes with a professional screenwriter, or clerk for a particular judge. A mentor may be young or old, male or female, highly educated or illiterate, rich, poor, from a different race or ethnic background, or have a different sexual orientation from yours.

How to Choose a Mentor

The most important quality in a mentor is his or her integrity. It's important when becoming involved in mentorship to check out the person's spirit and intentions. Get references. Talk to others who have dealt with or have a relationship with that person. Preventive measures don't take a long time and they can save you the embarrassment and even pain of situations that involve exploitation, sexual harassment, or other treachery.

Be Cautious and Aware

Some mentors and gurus send off "bad vibes" right off the bat. Notice if they are "touchy feely" with you, or overly probing about your circumstances. Body language, eye contact, and the promise of "instant intimacy" are clues as to what the relationship will be. People who are biased, competitive, who are wrapped up in themselves with no sense of others, who can't give backing, who lie, or who exploit your ideas are not true mentors.

You know the expression, do they "walk the walk"? In other words, are they just talk, or do they do what they say? Almost everyone has role models and mentor relationships, even if they haven't before thought of them in that way. For example, Beth, a graduate student in German studies, told us that bravery for her is "standing up for what you believe in and just going with it." Her role model is St. Agnes. "I remember reading about St. Agnes in Bible study. She ended up being flogged and had to walk through the streets naked, because she was standing up for something. That's pretty courageous."

A List of Inspiration

In your journal or on a sheet of paper you can hang up somewhere, make a list of people you most admire. They can be from real life or fictional characters, but they must speak to your dreams and desires.

Next, create a list of potential mentors. Write down everything you know about them. What are their most admirable qualities?

Kate and the Artist's Way: A Brave New Path

Kate is a poet, playwright, musician, and a writing professor. For twenty-five years, she has been writing plays and musicals. The arts drive and animate her life. Kate doesn't buy into the myth that artists have to be poor to be good. Bravery to her is "consciously choosing to be a serious artist in the American culture and being able to make a long-range commitment to an idea or project."

She has had three mentors and an inspirational muse, namely Shakespeare, "the world's greatest playwright," because he was able "to invent great male and female characters and to get to the truth about humanity." For Kate, mentorship is a relationship of mutual respect and understanding, and one where the mentor chooses who is going to be her or his protégée. "It doesn't work the other way around. A mentor expects great things from you, no matter what the context, whether it's in a fourth-grade art class or a performance at Carnegie Hall. My mentors all had a strong presence. They made contact with me frequently and they encouraged my creativity."

Kate's first mentor, a high school English teacher, was "passionate about literature," and the next, a music teacher, was "madly in love with music. They both taught me to take creative, imaginative work as the most serious business in the world. Their input was much more important and influential than anything later on."

In graduate school, Kate met John Malcolm Brinnin, the distinguished poet who brought Dylan Thomas to America. He had a deep respect for the craft of poetry and, again, encouraged Kate to take her passion for writing seriously. "I remember he had this sweet cottage on the water in Duxbury," she said, "where the class would meet and talk about poetry in a very human way. He was always pushing me to the next level, pushing the envelope of creativity. He wore a suit and a bow tie to teach. He was very classy, old school. He taught me how to work with images and their energies."

Mentors help you find the building blocks for success. They are the people upon whom you rely as you're pursuing your dreams. Mentors can empower your career and professional life, but their power and wisdom may also be instrumental in deepening your relationships with your partner, enhancing your relationships with parents and siblings, with your children, and with your friends. Mentors will help accelerate your progress and breathe life into your dreams.

Chapter 11

Change Your Thinking to Change Your World

*Every human being's central need is to express herself to
the world as she really is—in word, in gesture, in behavior,
in art—in every genuine expression, beginning with the baby's cry.*

—Alice Miller

Dynamic strategy No. 11 is to examine the way you think, to look at how you react to problems, and to change your self-talk and thought processes to positive, self-affirming visions. Change your thinking and revamp how you talk to yourself, and you will change your world and your voice. The outer world is a reflection of the world inside you. If your inner world is working well and in good order, the outer world will follow suit.

Maximize Your Brain Power

History, culture, and scholarship have long proclaimed cultural myths that simply aren't true. For example, a common myth is that women exclusively have a strong sense of intuition, relying on subjective rather than objective knowledge; and men solely reason their way through life and apply logic to solve their problems. The truth, however, is that some of the most intuitive people on Earth are men, and some of the most rational thinkers are women.

The problem is that cultural myths will infiltrate into and become part of your belief system. Your beliefs then are supported through *selective perception*, the natural tendency to recognize behaviors that fit your beliefs and reinforce them, while inadvertently omitting behaviors that don't fit into your beliefs and stereotypes.

Your *socialization*, the way you were brought up to think, is the starting point for determining your beliefs and your thinking. Your *beliefs* shape the attitudes, mindsets, or positions that you take about general and specific situations. Your *attitudes* affect your feelings and emotions, which determine your everyday behavior and actions.

If you were raised, for example, to believe that women are intuitive and emotional, you may have been encouraged to develop a subjective sense of thinking. That is, you rely less on objective information, and instead "feel if something is right" or "sense the truth" or "just know the truth inside of you." This kind of thinking, however, dubbed subjectivism or "subjective knowing" in the breakthrough study *Women's Ways of Knowing* (Belenky, Clinchy, Goldberg, et al. 1997), has proven to have silenced, thwarted, and limited the development of many women's voices and minds.

Ways of "Knowing"

All people have intuition, men as well as women, and all people possess reasoning powers, logic, imagination, a conscious and a subconscious mind. Well-integrated individuals have both acute intuitive powers and scientifically trained minds that understand each and every nuance and detail. Some people are more specialized. They may have a highly developed imagination or be able to construct highly sophisticated rhetorical arguments.

If you exercise your intuition just as you would a muscle, you will develop the skill of intuitive knowing, a prerequisite to bravery. Exercise the powers of reason and logic, and you will develop the skill of critical thinking, which also will enhance and augment your bravery. Your intuition and imagination tell you that it's time to assert the strength of your courage and to forge ahead, while your reasoning powers and logic help you implement the steps toward realizing your dreams and goals.

As a brave woman you must bypass the cultural myths and types of thinking that hold you back. Your conscious mind is fully equipped to explore, challenge, contest, undo, deconstruct, recreate, develop, pose, articulate, reason, and think through anything or any area you choose to challenge and investigate. Your inner voice and subconscious mind (addressed fully in chapter 12) illuminate the landscape of your possibilities and allow you to see the world around you with clear fresh eyes.

Subjective Conclusions

One way to know something is through your "gut" or how you feel about it at a primal level. You may say, "My gut tells me that I shouldn't go on this trip with this person. There's something that doesn't feel right about it." There's nothing rational about that intuition, and yet you're receiving information from somewhere inside you. It's almost a visceral, bodily sensation. You sense, sniff, or taste that there's something not quite right about a situation.

Objective Conclusions

Another way of gleaning knowledge is from an outside source or authority. For example, you may consult the dictionary to find the meaning of a word and discover its definition next to a particular entry. In this case, you're trusting in the authority of a publisher or the editor who supplies the information. In addition, you may research the word by looking at its etymology, from what language it was derived, or its history; how was it used in the 1600s? What are the synonyms and antonyms? In other words, you let your mind and imagination play with and interact with the "facts."

The Power of Language

You can never underestimate the power of language. It is totally transformative, positively or negatively. The way you talk to yourself creates and affects everything about you.

Make Over Your Self-Talk

Your self-talk or inner dialogue sets the tone for how you feel, think, and behave. Feeling frazzled, stressed, urgent, or anxious hampers your optimum functioning and interferes with or blocks the pathways that link your conscious awareness to your inner self. In chapter 12, you will tap into the powers of your subconscious mind and inner world. Before that, however, you need to make over your thinking or how you manage your mind.

Mind management, learning how to manage your self-talk in effective ways, can drive away discouragement and transform anxiety into inner strength and peace. When you improve your self-talk, you feel better and do better. A clearer channel opens to your inner self. The static that comes from faulty thinking or emotional upset and overload makes it difficult to be sensitive and open to your inner mind and voice. The pathway between your conscious mind and inner knowing determines your success or failure in life, and shapes how much courage you can gather to push through your obstacles and achieve your goals.

Negative Self-Talk

Negative self-talk is when you put yourself down or unjustifiably exaggerate the negatives either about yourself, your situation, or others. Usually self-talk is an inner monologue, yet it also can be talking to yourself or someone else out loud. Catch yourself in the act and put a stop to putting yourself down.

Negative self-talk creates unnecessary static and interferes with the powerful messages you receive from your inner voice or inner core. It interferes with your ability to perceive yourself, the world, and others with clarity and precision.

Proactive Not Reactive

As a brave woman, you take the initiative and are proactive, not reactive, to the circumstances of your life and to the way that you are. *Proactive* is when you *take* the initiative and let others react to you. You take responsibility to turn things around. You create a different way of thinking and knowing, a different way of feeling, and a different way of doing. *Reactive* is letting things happen *to* you and then reacting.

Increase Awareness

The first step to being more proactive is to be more aware of your usual responses to problems. For example, do you overreact and automatically think "catastrophe"? Do you underreact and bury your feelings and concerns? Develop the habit of monitoring your reactions by mentally stepping outside your response. Determine which, if any, of your reactions are reflexive or knee-jerk and automatic, and which ones are self-defeating or detract from your ability to think clearly.

For instance, are you a drama queen? Is your customary reaction to a problem to blow up, fly off the handle, panic, or become enraged? Perhaps when something happens, you automatically find someone other than yourself to blame. You hit the car in front of you and ask, "Dear, why did you make me do that?"

Negative or defeatist self-talk is defective software that keeps your mental computer from running optimally and effectively. To get rid of this program, you have to know what you're looking for. In many cases, it's been with you for so long that it feels perfectly natural.

It's important to listen to what you're saying to yourself. Are you being overly critical of yourself, of others, or of your circumstances? Are you being practical? Many of us have an inner dialogue consisting of irrational beliefs, thoughts, and feelings. Although these thoughts have no basis in fact, and can't be proven, they persist and negatively affect our perceptions and our feelings. When you find yourself in conversation, stop and pause. Use the momentary lapse in response to become aware of the automatic tape you run inside your head.

You can unlearn the way that you talk to yourself, and replace negative or distorted thinking with bold, courageous, self-affirming thoughts. If your self-talk is unreasonably harsh and critical, it's crucial not to allow the negativity in your mind to get the best of you. Persistent negative self-talk distorts your reality. Clearer thinking requires mental training. Become aware of *how* you think about things not just about what you are thinking.

It's a Habit

Negative self-talk is habitual and well ingrained. It is so automatic and so much a part of you that it may completely eclipse your objective awareness. Do you ever stop to think about what you're thinking? Do any of the monologues below repeat endlessly in your head?

- "I just can't do anything right."
- "With my luck I'm sure to fail."
- "I'm so stupid."
- "I just can't get my act together."
- "I have no talent."
- "I'm an imposter."
- "I can't stand myself."
- "That's impossible."

- "I don't have what it takes."

- "I'm a loser."

Gain Control and Diffuse the Impact

As you become aware of your negative self-talk, the next step is to gain greater control of these thoughts and diffuse their impact on your life.

Make a List. Start by writing a list of your negative self-talk statements to create greater awareness of what you're telling yourself and to interrupt the negative cycle of thoughts. Writing your self-talk down makes it psychologically more manageable for you—you simply won't feel as overwhelmed when you see your negative self-talk thoughts on paper.

Say Stop. If your inner dialogue is self-critical say **STOP!** out loud. Draw a picture of the word or a stop sign or any other relevant image on a notepad or computer screen. Next, create a more positive dialogue—either in your mind or by writing it down on paper—to end the reflexive and negative dialogue.

Make a vow. Promise yourself that you'll stop using self-defeating thoughts and practice the steps you learned above. Be consistent and diligent, but don't strive for perfection. The hardest part is beginning. As you get rid of these tired, habitual thinking patterns, perhaps for the first time, the self-defeating thoughts will try to reassert themselves. This will lessen with time and practice.

Your next step is to fill the vacuum that housed your negative self-talk with positive more uplifting thoughts.

Positive Self-Talk

Create positive self-talk to replace the negative self-talk. All of your new self-talk must be in the *present tense*. Future tense thinking does not create change, but present tense does. Examples of positive self-talk include:

- "I'm awesome!"

- "I've got personality."

- "I'm intelligent."

- "I'm blessed with many abilities."

- "I feel good about myself. People respect me."

- "I'm unstoppable."

- "I'm determined and successful."

- "I manage my thoughts well."

- "I think clearly and effectively."

- "I am successful at what I do, because I'm successful as a person."

- "I have the courage to do what I must do to get where I must go."

- "I control my thoughts, my life, and my actions."

- "I control my circumstances, they do not control me."

On paper, write or type out some personalized, positive self-talk statements that best reflect your circumstances. Visualize your brilliant moments, your courage under fire, and succeeding against the odds. It is effective to record what you have written on a cassette tape. Play this tape as you prepare for the day and at various intervals throughout the day. Hearing your new self-talk becomes reinforcement, as the repetition ingrains positive self-talk into your consciousness. Remember that new thoughts create new beliefs, which change your attitudes. New attitudes, in turn, affect your feelings and allow you to express your bravery and courage through new behaviors and actions.

Be Warned: Stay Positive

Be aware of the negative and self-sabotaging self-talk that may come up while doing this assignment. You might say to yourself, "This is ridiculous, I'm too old and too set in my ways to change," or "This is too simple or silly to work." You might say, "Get real! I know what I feel and what my situation is like. Why should I fool myself with thinking that that doesn't reflect any of this."

The difficulty is that you allow your thinking, feeling, and self-talk to reflect what you feel and what you see in the moment. In other words, you allow events to shape and create your thoughts instead of allowing your thoughts to shape the events and experiences in your life.

As your self-talk changes, you'll see yourself differently. You will feel differently as your perception of everything around you changes. This will happen because your environment is a reflection of the sum total of your experiences, your beliefs, and your thoughts.

You're Like That Already

Think and act as if you've already accomplished your goals and you are the person that you've always wanted to be. Remember, in time, your outer reality will reflect your inner thinking—it's really that simple. If your thinking always reflects your outer reality, nothing will change for you.

Rethinking the Ways You Think

The following ways of thinking get you into trouble over and over again, mainly because it's very difficult to notice these faulty approaches to situations, people, and problems.

Mind Reading

Mind reading is the belief that allows you to believe that you can know what other people are thinking. You may become falsely confident about mind reading if there have been times when you've guessed other's motives and what they're thinking correctly, because you know them well. However, in many cases, you interpret what a person says or does by imputing erroneous, irrelevant, or unworthy motives to what they're thinking and doing. Mind reading leads to false accusations and hurt feelings. The opposite occurs, too. You can give a person more credit than is due and consider their motives more genuinely sincere than they truly are.

Black and White Thinking

With *black and white thinking*, you fail to see the "gray" in peoples' actions and situations, and believe you always are faced with all-or-nothing predicaments. That is, you don't acknowledge the middle ground of anything. Situations and people are either good or bad, possible or impossible, successful or failures, happy or unhappy, etc.

Perfectionists tend to veer into black and white thinking. For example, if a performance is not totally perfect, then it's totally flawed, or if you don't get an "A" on an exam or paper, then you've failed. This thinking creates unrealistic pressure to succeed beyond the bounds of reason and "reality," and frustration, disappointment, and self-condemnation set in.

As a brave woman you refuse to view situations in absolutes. You expand your vision to see the vast complexity of things. You are wise in the ways of the world and regarding human nature.

Exaggerated Thinking

When you embellish anything about yourself or others, you are employing *exaggerated thinking*. Sometimes you may do this for dramatic effect or to get your point across in a memorable manner. In many cases, however, you exaggerate your thinking to fit a preconceived notion of how you should think and feel about something or somebody, including yourself.

When you want to feel better or worse about someone or something, you may exaggerate their qualities and motives to better fit your emotions. Exaggerated thinking has two components: *idealistic* and *catastrophic*.

Idealistic Thinking

Thinking in storybook terms—such as situations ending "happily ever after" or insisting on seeing certain people as "larger than life" and not as the mere flawed mortals that they really are—is *idealistic thinking*. This type of thinking stems from wish fulfillment: desperately wanting to live in an always secure and safe world with few disappointments and shocks. When you find that the emperor's new clothes are no clothes at all, you become deeply disappointed and disillusioned by people and circumstances. The brave woman tells the emperor he's naked.

Catastrophic Thinking

The opposite of idealistic thinking on the exaggerated thinking continuum is *catastrophic thinking*. Catastrophic thinking is the "downside" of exaggeration: the horror film that plays in your head. This kind of thinking requires an active imagination and stems from deep fears and insecurities. It is expressed as anger or dread and is set off by perceived threats to your well-being and even your sense of survival.

When you feel that you can't control a threatening situation, you *catastrophize* it. That is, you inflate the consequences of an event and experience an unmistakable sense of doom and feel that "all is lost." For example, a spouse is at the receiving end of her partners' anger. Instead of seeing the anger as attached to an issue of miscommunication, stress, or hurt that needs to be addressed, she views his anger as a prelude to physical violence and becomes scared that her partner will imminently attack her, even though her partner has no history of physical violence.

In this case, the exaggerated catastrophic thinking may be a displacement of growing up in a family where her father expressed anger and then was prone to hit his wife and kids. The partner fuses the verbal anger that she sees in her spouse with the violence she saw in her father. Without realizing, she is unable to separate her present experiences from the intimidations of her past. Her catastrophic thinking becomes generalized and is automatically ignited whenever she is confronted with an angry person.

This example of catastrophic thinking continues unabated until the partner gains psychological insight into why she becomes so deathly afraid for her safety whenever someone becomes angry with her.

Understanding that her dread, fear, and catastrophic thinking arose from her past experiences serves as a corrective measure and diffuses the intensity of emotion and thinking that she feels. This requires that her inner voice of reason speak to her.

First she asks herself why she experiences such intense feeling and such catastrophic thoughts when her spouse has never harmed her. The inner voice residing within her unconscious mind brings forth the memories of why she reacts as she does and connects with her reasoning powers. It can create a liberating insight. To understand something is the beginning of being able to influence and master it. When you give meaning and shape to what baffles you, it is drained of the strength to cause you harm.

As a brave woman, you don't exaggerate and embellish on what you think, feel, and observe. You see people and situations for what they are, know what you're faced with, and work within the framework of *what is*, not the imposition of a wish fulfillment on reality. It takes bravery and inner security to see people and situations in this unadorned, realistic way.

Another example is the partner who goes over the spending budget. The more frugal partner views this excess with alarm and starts to think of the disastrous consequences of this overspending: "We won't be able to pay the bills this month. Once he starts spending money, he won't be able to stop. For sure we'll wind up in bankruptcy."

This kind of escalated, catastrophic thinking increases the fear of losing everything, the insecurities well up, and fear and anger get the best of her. She starts to think that her partner is irresponsible and doesn't care about their situation or future. She generalizes and starts to see her partner as sabotaging their best-laid plans. They're off to the "mind races," as the situation now grows worse before it is better. To move past exaggerated thinking patterns is to deal with fears and insecurities that relate to basic survival issues.

Minimizing Thinking

Minimizing is trying to lessen the impact of an event or its consequences or simply not paying attention to a significant situation. You simply make the significant less important in your mind. This way of thinking reduces the anxiety and stress connected with something important that you're facing. It's also a way of reducing the emotional impact of a disappointment or failure.

For example, if an interview for your dream job didn't go well, you could say that the job really wasn't as important as you originally had thought.

Minimizing causes you to avoid difficult and important tasks and responsibilities. This mental mechanism works to reduce immediate unpleasantries and stress, but at the cost of greater pressure and upset in the future.

An example is the student who is about to take a major exam. Although she should spend the evening studying, she instead goes out with friends. By minimizing what's truly important to her, she faces failing the test and her course.

As a brave woman you meet your responsibilities head on. You know that to minimize and avoid what must be done now only creates greater stress and hardship in the future. You see things for what they are, never minimizing the importance of what you do, but never inflating its importance either. You strive for a balanced perspective. You understand the consequences of actions taken and not taken.

Selective Perception

With *selective perception* you only perceive what you already believe about something. This kind of thinking occurs when an investment in a belief or course of action is so great that it's difficult to make a course correction when new information presents itself. The more time and energy you've invested in something, the more reluctant you are to give it up. Selective perception strengthens the belief and keeps us on course, although it may be counterproductive and hurtful.

The negative effects of selective perception occur when you refuse to see that something that has been so much a part of you is no longer a healthy situation: a relationship, a job, habits, an overall way of living. For example, you could be in a job that no longer has much meaning to you; it pays the bills, but it doesn't offer the creative stretch that you require in this new phase of your life. Still you stick with it.

The thought of changing jobs may be too upsetting and threatening to you. You've invested so much time and energy in your position that you don't want all this time to go to waste. So you look at the perks, the nice people you work with, your insurance and health benefits, and the flexible hours that the boss allows you. Yet you know that something is wrong and you can't quite put your finger on it. You may not be fully conscious of your predicament and why you feel the way you do because your time and energy is being spent thinking about the benefits of your job, not in thinking that it's time to move on.

Selective perception causes you to be stuck and to hold on to outmoded ways of thinking and doing. You only choose to do and only choose to see that which makes you secure and comfortable. Getting out of the comfort zone, even though it's unsatisfying and painful, is too frightening. You would be faced with the unknown, faced with surprises, faced with learning to do things differently, faced with an unpredictability that stirs up untold anxiety and fear.

As a brave woman you refuse to hold on to the old and outmoded, realizing that change is your salvation. Change sparks your creativity and your ability to bring out the best that you have within yourself. You discover that novelty and unpredictability create your greatest challenges and embrace the new, for it reflects where you are now.

As a brave woman you say goodbye: so long to work that is meaningless to you, relationships that are toxic and destructive, and places that are stifling.

Overgeneralization Thinking or Totalizing

Overgeneralization or *totalizing* occurs when a single event becomes generalized into other events. The thought is, "If it happened once it will happen again." If the event is a pleasant one, this isn't much of an issue. But suppose the event is a negative one, then what? For example, a partner may say, "He *never* gives me credit for anything I do" or "She's *always* belittling my character" or "You *never* care about my feelings" or "You're *always* so irresponsible." These sweeping generalizations occur after one or only a few isolated incidences, and they create a distorted view of a person whose character flaws become magnified and the anger and miscommunication intensify.

As a brave woman you understand that people can disappoint you and make regrettable mistakes, but as you get to know people who are important in your life you understand that many of the incidences are isolated, rare occurrences that don't speak of the person as a whole. You forgive and forget because you know that you will exhibit to your partner—and hopefully be forgiven—your own failings.

Personalization

Personalization assumes that other people's actions are aimed directly at you. This thinking fails to account for people being motivated or compelled by their own agenda and not because of you. People prone to this kind of thinking tend toward being self-involved or suspicious of other people's motives or simply down right paranoid.

You find yourself at a business meeting discussing ways to improve company productivity with your supervisor. "Great idea!" he says. "I'll pass it up to the president." A memo comes back from the president stating that the plan, as good as it is, can't be implemented at this time. You start thinking, "He really doesn't like me. In fact, he doesn't like anything I do. What other reason could there be?"

Thinking like this can cause you to feel resentful and unappreciated. You never take into account that there may be a business reason why your idea can't be used at this time. Instead, by taking it personally, you put on mental blinders that keep you from seeing this as a business strategy, not as a way of expressing dislike of you. You begin to dislike the president and perhaps others in the chain of command because no one thought your idea was important enough to go to bat for you. You're soured, disillusioned, and angry, yet no one has a clue as to what you're feeling, because no one sees you as being wronged. And all of this unnecessary upset and hurt feelings are happening to you simply because you have *personalized* an impersonal decision.

Thinking that all that happens is directed at you causes you to be vigilant and untrusting in your relationships. You feel that life is a battle between you and the rest of the world. It's tough to let your hair down or turn your back to people when you habitually think this way.

As a brave woman you learn that people's actions don't mean that they have an ax to grind with you if they don't see or do things your way. You realize that many people are trying to work on issues and projects and to reach solutions to problems irrespective of the personalities involved. In knowing yourself as you do, you are able to have good insight into people and situations, so you don't waste your time thinking that something is of a personal nature when it is not.

However, you do understand that some people may be controlling and competitive with you and may *personalize* certain situations and issues. You are able to draw the distinction because you're not reading into people's behavior that which is not directly expressed to you, as it would be if the behavior *was* a personal affront.

As a brave woman you see the barriers erected against your progress, in the workplace, and in your personal life, but you don't become a victim of it. You right injustices by taking actions that empower you, that move you toward your destiny. You understand that people can be threatened by your success and would seek to stop you. You discover that even the personal cannot always be taken personally. The *personal* issue or criticism of you is really the problem of the criticizer.

When you view people and situations in this way you don't *personalize* and are not trapped by another's negative feelings or actions toward you. As a brave woman you move on and put your energies into your agenda for success and fulfillment.

As a brave woman you know that your journey is only as fine as the work you do on yourself. You discover who you are as you look at the way you think and try to correct behaviors that hurt you. You harness your energy and bravery in the service of others by your example, influence, and humanity. You temper your thinking and create a balanced self-empowered life.

This chapter has suggested that what you think about yourself and how you see others and your problems directly affects who you are. In other words, you shape and construct your reality based on how you mentally frame your sense of self and the world. A brave woman can easily switch between the intuitive knowledge of a visionary and the critical thought process, logic, and reason of a scientist. She doesn't shrink from, but rather enjoys a mental challenge, and she rejects the notion that there's any definitive relationship between gender and brainpower.

Chapter 12

Listen to the Brave New You

Live from Your Essential Core

Courage is the price that life extracts for granting peace.

—Amelia Earhart

You have now revealed all but one of the babushka's outer shells. As you open this last doll, nestled inside her, you will see the smallest and last babushka. She has the same face and colorful outfit as the others, but this one is different because she is made of solid wood and can't be pulled apart. Pick her up and feel the difference. This doll is unique, the original prototype for all her larger sisters. She is your touchstone.

The solid little piece of painted wood symbolizes your brave eternal self, the essence of your being. She is your center in the midst of chaos. Now meet her. You may have been out of touch with her for a very long time. Your sense of inner identity comes from this source. She is the voice inside you, she is with you at this moment, she has always been there, and she always will be. Your bravery emanates from this core.

Dynamic strategy No. 12 is discovering the articulation of your essential self that becomes real and palpable when you tune into the clear, directed, honest voice of conscience and inner direction inside you. A woman's bravery emanates from here and directs her path. Inspired lives derive their lifeblood from this intensely personal and powerful source, which comes alive from spending time alone, planning creative life strategies, contemplating your past, visualizing your future, daydreaming, and writing down your goals, musings, and secret desires in your journal.

Your Sense of Psyche

Your inner world of psyche, that is, your mind combined with your memories, sensations, and feelings, is an ever-changing environment—a kaleidoscope of shifting moods, colors, images, feelings, thoughts, hints, and intimations. Each woman's inner life is unique, its sounds and signals differ. Some inner voices whisper or speak loudly, others ripple through a woman's consciousness cajoling her into awareness. As the spool of consciousness unwinds inside you, you inhabit a world of feelings, memories, and sensations. You process experiences not always aware that you knit together your past and present feelings. You talk to yourself, maybe unaware that you're engaged in this activity.

Without becoming too philosophical, ask yourself how you experience your sense of psyche or self. You may not monitor your moods, and, in many instances, what you feel may suddenly come bolting out from nowhere—it's inexplicable. A self is invisible and yet you know it's there, speaking your thoughts, muttering your concerns, creating your fantasies and dreams, driving your emotions and reactions. The brave woman reflects on her thought processes and moods. Do you sense your innermost self as a voice or as feelings, or maybe as a picture? Do you observe your thoughts and watch your mind at play?

Heighten Your Sense of Self-Awareness

A heightened sense of self-awareness is a part of your inner knowing. It's the observation of yourself in the acts of thinking, knowing, and perceiving. Perhaps you've been too busy observing and being seduced by events outside of yourself, losing track of your inner voice and, therefore, your identity and sense of self. The *epiphany* or the revelation of inner voice illuminates your unique sense of being. It gives you direction and offers you a glimpse of an invisible world beyond what you've been taught to believe, beyond "facts," beyond the myths posing as cultural reality. It transcends the "social imprints" in our brain. Your inner voice is a knowing that is both transsocial and transcultural. It is deep, unshakable, and liberating. The ground zero and core of your "humanness," this sound is a primal awareness that cuts though your emotional and psychological restraints and brings you into the fullness of your being and life.

But what exactly is this inner voice, this inner knowing? In the act of being busy, always doing, meeting time lines and responsibilities, it's hard to connect with it.

Different Sounds of the Inner Voice

Each of the women below represents different stages of self-awareness. Some are familiar with their inner voice, others have recently come upon it and are just learning how to listen and respond to their inner signals, still others routinely seek counsel and guidance by going within, turning their attention and their conscious mind to what's happening inside of them.

Megan: When all is quiet, and I'm alone, I have the clearest, strongest sense of my voice. Courage is listening to that voice and honoring it.

Carey: When you're a writer, you're constantly being taught that somewhere inside you there is a very directed, honest voice. If you could just listen in, if you just tune in, then it might just direct your life somehow. That is what full-time living is all about.

Sara: My inner voice is usually so loud that I don't have a choice not to listen to it.

Trina: I'm a good singer. My voice is very strong when I sing or when I'm with my friends, but when I'm alone, it's hard to find. My bravery comes from somewhere deep in my soul.

Erin: Silence was such an issue in my childhood. I was sexually molested by my stepfather for several years and didn't say a word about it until I was sixteen and had been in therapy for a year. I learned to set boundaries and trust in the existence of my own voice.

Angela: When I began to become comfortable in my own skin, my inner voice became louder and louder. It's easy to be yourself and stick up for yourself when you can hear your inner voice.

Amy: I believe I live from the inside out. I voice my thoughts and base my actions on what's going on inside me. I don't hide them. People who act from the outside are trying to give others what they think they want instead of what they have to offer. You need to do something about your inside and then your outer world will change.

Joan: A Brave New Path

"Most of my friends are listening to Prozac instead of their core," said Joan, an avid mountain climber from the Northwest. "My core guides my life." Joan, who has always thought of herself as "different," makes that place inside her "my focal point." Forced to grow up on her own because of family circumstances (her father died when she was an adolescent and her mother was someone who needed to be taken care of herself), Joan's senses grew stronger and more keen as she struggled to survive.

After her father's death, Joan felt compelled to replace him with another male. She agreed to marry because she thought it was "the right thing to do." Over the course of their engagement, Joan started to experience debilitating migraine headaches. She consulted a neurologist who found nothing wrong, but directed her attention to her engagement ring: "I see you are wearing an engagement ring. Does this have anything to do with the headaches?" Joan became furious and thought he was trespassing in a nonmedical area, saying things he shouldn't say.

A few months later, Joan broke off the engagement and the headaches stopped. Now she knows her nervous system was sending her loud and clear messages about the decision she had made to marry. "That time my core spoke in migraine headaches. I guess it had to because I wasn't listening. After that day, I have tried not to go against what my core is telling me. When I do, I always regret it."

Joan conceptualizes what she calls her "core" as a primal, emotional field with a language all it's own. "It's something you have to fine-tune," she says, "and it only emerges when you know who you are. It's in your whole being, like DNA. When you don't know who you are, there's no core. Instead, you're jealous or hooked into materials things.

"I always knew what kind of woman I wanted to be. That image always has been in my mind. Now, I'm changing my priorities to make that inner vision of myself a reality. It's a thought process. You begin with the vision or the mental picture, change the colors, sharpen the focus, and view the home movies in your mind's eye. At fifty-five years old, I have never been happier, because I only listen to my core."

Joan's suggestion—to create a visualization of who and what you want to be—is the starting point for creating a relationship between your inner and outer worlds. As Joan said: "You let the inside out and the outside in to create a vision of what you want." You will find visualization techniques and guides at the end of this chapter so you can begin to create home movies of your life. There is a long-standing philosophical tradition, beginning with Plato and being voiced in this century by motivational writers and speakers: "You become what you think about."

Identify and Befriend Your Internal Voices

The Buddhist nun Pema Chödron (2000) makes a distinction between what the Tibetans call *sem*, the small mind, and *rikpa*, the larger mind. *Sem* is your self-talk (discussed at length in chapter 11) and *rikpa*, or "brightness," is the larger, brave mind. It is your core or your sense of inner knowing.

"Sem is what we experience as discursive thoughts, a stream of chatter that's always reinforcing an image of ourselves. Rikpa literally means 'intelligence' or 'brightness.' Behind all the planning and worrying, behind all the wishing and wanting, picking and choosing, the unfabricated, wisdom mind of rikpa is always there. Whenever we stop talking to ourselves, rikpa is continually there" (27).

The power, passion, and bravery you express unfolds in direct proportion to knowing who you are. To know yourself and your abilities is to be grounded in creating your life with your handiwork, your creativity, your talents, your wishes, and your dreams.

You are the one who must fully live your life. No one else can live it for you or tell you what your true mission and passions are. Only you know, because your inner knowing speaks as your voice within, the voice of conscience, the voice that tells you where you should be in this world.

Query Yourself and Ask the Right Questions

Inner knowing starts with a conscious awareness about yourself, your reactions and feelings, and the thoughts that speak to your wishes and dreams regarding your future. As a brave woman, you are a student of life, you observe people and situations, assimilate experiences, and try not to prejudge all that you witness.

Consult with yourself, check out how you feel and react in situations and toward other people. Observe *how* you think, not just what you think. Ask yourself questions that may not have immediate answers. Let the questions germinate within your unconscious mind. Suddenly, when doing something else or nothing at all, you'll have an "aha!" experience. The answer will be clear. You'll know and understand that which was before unclear. The answer will liberate you to the point where you needn't—and, in fact, can't—go back into the darkness of the unknown.

Your journey of self-discovery rests on the ability to ask yourself the right questions. The better your questions, the better the answers. The kinds of questions you ask yourself determine the quality and helpfulness of your answers. You want meaningful answers, answers that are productive, empowering, and that ignite your passion and courage. As a brave woman, go beyond questions that seek answers only to your problems. Pose questions that set the groundwork for your new life.

An Inner Journey of Self-Discovery: An Exercise

Your inner journey of self-discovery mainly consists of questions that you ask about yourself and your circumstances. The questions below are a starting point. As you consciously try to answer them, new, more helpful, and definitive questions will come to mind. With practice, the quality of your questions—and hence your answers—will improve. Increasingly, you want to be more proactive and less reactive to the circumstances of your life, creating the vision, purpose, and passion that will make your life a work of art.

It is extremely important to write down all of your questions and the answers. First, it will decrease stress and anxiety caused by trying to keep everything in your head. Second, you'll find your answers don't disappear just when you thought you had a handle on them, which is a frequent occurrence when you have an insight or revelation. Lastly, when you write out your problem, you'll see it in a different light and it will become more manageable.

1. Why is it vitally important for you to learn more about yourself? List a minimum of ten reasons.

2. Why is it essential for you to work toward your dreams? List a minimum of ten reasons.

3. Why is bravery crucial to your success in life? Fill the page or the computer screen with your reasons; you have many more then you realize.

4. What type of person will you become by learning more about yourself? Write down how you'll feel, how you'll relate to people, what you'll look like, where you'll live, what material objects you'll possess, what you'll do to help people in a healthy beneficial way. Next, create a vision in your mind of this person you've described. Make this "picture" as vivid as possible. *See* what you are doing and *feel* the wonderful emotions you are experiencing.

5. What rewards will you reap from the vision that you've created? (The vision in your mind will ignite your bravery and you will become that vision.)
   Read your answers to the above questions daily to continually fuel your bravery and passion for what you want to accomplish.

6. What must happen for you to feel successful? Write everything that comes to your mind without censoring or judging your answers.

7. What is the one thing that you love doing more than anything else? Why do you enjoy it? What kind of person do you think is attracted to the one thing you love doing the most?

8. Where do you see yourself a year from now?

9. Where do you see yourself five years from now?

10. Where do you see yourself ten years from now?

Your inner journey consists of questions that need to be answered consciously—thinking about them and brainstorming for solutions—or unconsciously where the solution and insight to your problem resides with your inner core. Many people who answer the last three questions see very few changes in their circumstances as they project one, five, and ten years into the future. This merely means that you are a bit stuck in your thinking and in your growth process. In this case, it is even more important that you create and carry a clear vision of how you will be and what you will be doing and accomplishing. The bravery, energy, and motivation to create the future comes directly from the clarity of your vision.

As a brave woman you know that if you don't grow as a person, you stagnate. You are always open to your inner journey, the rewards are great, and you wouldn't have your life any other way. Your inner journey clears the pathway to the outer one.

Depend on Your Unconscious Mind

There are different metaphors that people use to describe the *unconscious* mind. Some call it their higher self or power or superconscious, others call it their inner voice, still others call it their inner guide or even the inner whispering of their angel.

A word of warning: Your unconscious mind has the answers to your questions and for your life; however, you must always be a student of life and never become so self-reliant that you ignore the world around you and don't listen to others. Your unconscious mind creates situations where you *consciously* meet with people who share their wisdom and experiences with you. You must allow for that.

As social beings, we are interdependent and share with each other. We learn and become wiser from these interactive experiences. This is why mentors are such an important part of your brave journey (see chapter 10). You learn best from those who have been where you're going. Your unconscious mind provides answers from within and creates answers from without through a variety of our social experiences and personal interactions.

The Inner Oracle and How It Works

Ask your inner being or unconscious mind to solve or provide insight or clarification into certain vexing situations that are troubling you. At some point, when you least expect it, your inner voice will speak to you in the form of a feeling, or images or words, or as a revelation that creates a shift in your awareness, or it may come as an immediate solution.

Trust your inner voice to provide the answer and you will receive it. Interestingly, your inner voice may provide you your answer in an unexpected way, even through a fortuitous event. You may meet someone who will provide the answer that you seek, or you may find it in a book that will suddenly command your attention. You may find yourself going to an event that provides you with answers.

Time Sensitive Questions

You may have some pressing issues that need answers right away. Just ask your unconscious mind the question and tell it by when you need the answer. For example, "I want an answer to this problem by next Friday at 6 P.M." Your next step is to stop thinking consciously about solving the problem and let your inner core or unconscious mind work on it.

One caveat: Don't give your unconscious mind a false time line if you're not under any time pressure for an answer. To do so is to interfere *consciously* with your *unconscious* process because of impatience, fears, or insecurities, or the anxiety and dread of not knowing something fast enough. This will make it difficult to keep your channel to your unconscious mind as open as it can be, making it difficult to receive the answer that you need.

Dreaming of Answers

Certain questions that you ask yourself may take longer to answer than others. One of the best times to have your inner self work for you is when you're sleeping. Write down a question or create a list of questions (you can create a new list or use the list from earlier in the chapter) and ask your unconscious mind to work on them as you sleep. You'll wake up in the morning with an answer. Even if you don't consciously remember the answer, you can be assured that you are subconsciously beginning to work it through.

You may find that when you wake up you have the answers to some of your questions and not others—don't become disappointed or disheartened. There are times where your unconscious mind has a mind of its own as to when you'll have your revelation or answers to your issues and problems. You'll receive your answers when you are ready or the time is right, though this may be at odds with your need to know answers right away.

As a brave woman you trust that your unconscious mind will provide the answers that you seek at just the right time for you. Not any sooner or any later. You also trust in your *conscious faculties* when decisions and choices must be made right away with little time for contemplation.

Bold Immediate Decisions

When an important decision needs to be made immediately, you can't put off making the decision because you're waiting for your unconscious mind to provide the answer before you act. As a brave woman you have the courage and boldness to make conscious decisions immediately when situations demand it.

You trust that you've made the right decision; however, if it turns out to be wrong, you learn from the experience and understand that your decision is a reflection of your fallible humanity. Making mistakes is part of your growth as a brave woman: it increases your learning curve, keeps your ego in check, and humbles you, when necessary.

The Mind/Body Connection

This chapter thus far has explored the power of your inner self as the key to your bravery, personal change, and transformation. To create change, to sustain your ongoing commitment, requires energy and good physical health. What good is it to have the tools to change, the dreams to aspire to, and the lifestyle you want to live if you don't have the energy, stamina, and good physical health that it takes to be persistent, if not persevering, in achieving the life that you want.

As a brave woman you know that it is absolutely essential that you take care of your physical health and strive to improve it. You will accomplish more in a shorter period of time when your plans and inner knowing, your inner work, are in balance with a conscious application of behaviors that lead to your physical well-being and to behaviors that support your health. You'll find that you can sustain your activities, stick with your plans, and push through difficult roadblocks and obstacles far more effectively and easily if you optimize and sustain your body's functioning.

Your mood, energy level, and how you feel about yourself is directly related to how well you take care of your body and maintain your health through disciplined behavior. As a brave woman you don't allow this vitally important part of your life to lapse. You are knowledgeable about your body and how to keep it optimally functioning. Your good health habits become as automatic and as second nature to you as the work that you do with your inner self.

The Basics of Physical Exercise

It's been proven again and again that a mere fifteen to twenty minutes of exercise a day confers a greater sense of well-being, a healthy glow, and provides innumerable health benefits. Regular exercise, even a walk around your neighborhood, clears the mind, stimulates your subconscious, and distracts you from everyday or pressing problems. The exercise "high" you receive from an increase in endorphins can put you in an altered state of flow and deep meditation. Any repetitive physical act—rowing, running, walking (even on a treadmill), swimming, etc.—becomes Zen-like and hypnotic.

Workouts for Your Spirit

As a brave woman you will have pressure-packed days when stress is high, and your energy and tolerance are low. You may not have had enough sleep, you may not have eaten properly, or you may have had more to do in a given day than you had originally planned. Under these circumstances, facing tasks and responsibilities becomes more difficult, and solving problems seem more formidable than when you have more reserves and energy to draw upon.

On the days when you're feeling fatigued and not as clear or sharp and focused as you'd like to be, take the time to draw on the power of your unconscious mind to rejuvenate you.

Remember to Breathe

You will find the following exercise will rejuvenate you. You will experience renewed energy, greater enthusiasm, your fatigue will have evaporated, and your mind will be more at peace.

1. Sit down or lie down in a very comfortable position.

2. Close your eyes.

3. Take three deep diaphragmatic breaths. With each inhale, imagine that you are breathing in calm, peace, and relaxation. With each exhale, breathe out all tension, worry, and stress.

4. Next, breathe normally and rhythmically. As you begin to relax, try not to think of anything. Imagine you have stepped outside of yourself for a brief time, so that the necessary repairs can be done on your mind and body.

5. When the repair work has been done—usually within five to thirty minutes—you will experience the need to open your eyes. Depending on how tired you were prior to doing this exercise, you may take even more time.

As you use the power of your unconscious mind to bring forth the brave new you, you will become more determined and motivated to succeed. As you continue to repeat your "inner knowing" exercises, you become more proficient and effective in working with your unconscious mind. The more you do it, the better you will become at rejuvenating yourself.

Penelope: A Brave New Path

After a series of major losses, her second divorce, her parents' deaths, being laid off from work, and battling cancer, Penelope put away her unrealistic expectations about romance, how she should be loved, and how she should be on the material and career fast tracks. She simply let go and trusted herself to find a reason to get up every day. At forty-nine years old, she did "a radical intervention" on her life. Now, she has "my cat, my internal sense of values, my self, my friends, and my art."

As a professional child model, Penelope was required to be a responsible adult from age one. Her mother transformed her little daughter and son into runway models and a famous brother and sister act that appeared in fashion shows, lots of national television, and public dramas. "I had to jump into live television and improvise those skills at a very early age. My brother was the superstar, a reality that was hard to swallow, and we were 'geeks' as professional actor kids are and the object of other kids' derision."

Those taunts, the pain of rejection in show business, the work ethic, and her unhappy home life taught Penelope professional bravery: "You become inured to rejection and failure, you tend to become a people pleaser, and you give up your girlhood. I was a little adult and an immature baby inside. The other side is I got very strong and empathized with the real geeks. I've always had a wish to be five again."

In college, she was very brave, tough, rejected the good girl values, and "scared the shit out of men." She married what she describes as "an atypical bohemian. They left the country and traveled all through Southeast Asia with the attitude that "whatever we met up with, we could handle." Penelope lived in Japan for four years and returned to the States where she has held many jobs and had multiple careers.

Over the years, she has become more and more honest in her work, in her personal life, and in her art. Now as a university administrator, a potter, a sculptor, and a motivator, Penelope, at midlife, says what she wants and is who she was meant to be.

The Most Powerful Bravery

Having a reason to live and a meaningful life creates the most powerful bravery imaginable. All your channels are open to your life force. You are undaunted and unstoppable, and you feel so strongly about what you want to accomplish that when you hit roadblocks, you refuse to give up. Your desire and passion never waver, because your bravery is the driving force that brings you to your destination. You carry a vision of the future in your mind.

Anne Frank: A Brave Path

Writing the foreword of the diary kept by Anne Frank (1952), who died in a concentration camp three months short of her sixteenth birthday, two months before the liberation of Holland, Eleanor Roosevelt observed: "Sustained by her warmth and her wit, her intelligence and the rich resources of her inner life, Anne wrote and thought much of the time about things which very sensitive and talented adolescents without the threat of death will write . . ." (vii).

Anne Frank's bravery is timeless. Her courage, whetted by a sense of injustice, derived from her sense of self-possession and the knowledge, in her words, "That the final forming of a person's character lies in their own hands" (234). Anne Frank's words and experiences continue to affect people for many reasons, but mainly because what she wanted most was to be herself. Her song to life was written in her diary to her friend Kitty on Tuesday, April 11, 1944.

> I am becoming still more independent of my parents, young as I am. . . . My feeling for justice is immovable. . . . I know what I want, I have a goal, an opinion, I have a religion and love. Let me be myself and then I am satisfied. I know that I'm a woman, a woman of inward strength and courage. If God lets me live, I shall not remain insignificant. I shall work in the world and for mankind!

As the "approaching thunder" closed in around Anne Frank, she held on to her essential brave self and glimpsed her future as a writer. How could she imagine the impact of her words: "I have lots of courage," she wrote, "I always feel so strong and as if I can bear a great deal, I feel so free and young!"

Six decades or so later, although freedom reigns, the challenge for women to speak their minds and be themselves remains the same. In a culture that urges conformity, there is nothing more appealing than a woman striving to be an individual.

The brave woman inside has revealed herself to you. She will open up possibilities, bestow you with presence and authenticity, propel you toward your destiny, and lead you down paths you wouldn't before have dared to explore.

Bravery, as you have discovered, is not putting on armor or building defenses. Instead, it is shedding the layers of beliefs and defenses that prevent you from being yourself. The brave new you is vulnerable and daring—more self-possessed in mind and spirit than ever before. Women look to you for inspiration. Men who are secure with their own identity find you captivating. Your beliefs, values, and actions are in harmony. You know who you are, you know what you believe in, and you know how to convey those thoughts and ideals to the world. You test life's limits and recognize your gifts and abilities. You say what you mean and you truly are the brave new you.

Bibliography

Allen, Woody. 1989. *Crimes and Misdemeanors*. Orion Pictures. Film.

Ansay, H. Manette. 1999. *Vinegar Hill*. New York: William Morrow.

Austen, Jane. 1811. *Sense and Sensibility*. New York: Signet (1967).

———. 1816. *Emma*. New York: Penguin (1966).

Belenky, M., B. Clinchy, N. Goldberg, and J. Tarule. 1997. *Women's Ways of Knowing: The Development of Self, Voice, and Mind*. New York: Basic Books/Perseus.

Breathnach., S. 1995. *Simple Abundance: A Daybook of Comfort and Joy*. 1995. New York: Warner Books.

Cameron, Julia. 1992. *The Art ist's Way: A Spir i tual Path to Higher Cre ativ-ity*. New York: Tarcher/Putnam.

Campbell, Joseph. 1991. Interview by Bill Moyers. *Public Broadcasting System*, "The Power of Myth."

Chi cago, Judy. 1975. *Through the Flower: My Strug gle as a Woman Art ist*. New York: Penguin.

Chödron, Pema. 2000. *When Things Fall Apart: Heart Advice for Diffi cult Times*. Boston: Shambhala Publications.

Coles, Robert. 1998. *The Moral In tel li gence of Children*. New York: Random House.

Estes, Clara Pinkola. 1992. *Women Who Run With the Wolves: Myths and Stories of the Wild Woman Archetype*. New York: Ballantine.

Foster, Jodie. 1999. Interviewed by Larry King. CNN's Larry King Live. December 4.

Frank, Anne. 1952. *Anne Frank: The Diary of a Young Girl*. New York: Washington Square Press/Pocket.

Friedan, Betty. 1984. *The Feminine Mystique*. New York: Dell.

Ford, Deb bie. 1999. *The Dark Side of the Light Chasers: Reclaiming Your Power, Creativity, Brilliance, and Dreams*. New York: Riverhead Books/Peguin.

Frost, Robert. 1964. *Complete Poems of Robert Frost*. New York: Holt, Rhinehart, and Winston.

Gilligan, Carol. 1982. *In a Different Voice: Psychological Theory and Women's Development*. Cam bridge, Massachusetts: Har vard Uni ver sity Press.

Golden, Steph a nie. 1998. *Slaying the Mermaid: Women and the Cul ture of Sacrifice*. New York: Three Rivers Press.

Gordon, Shirley. 2001. Personal Communication. March 11.

Horner, M. S. 1972. "Toward an Understanding of Achievement Related Conflicts in Women." *Journal of Social Issues* 28.

Hutchinson, Kay Bayley. 2001. Interviewed by Greta Van Sustern. CNN's *The Point with Greta Van Sustern*. February 12.

Jong, Erica. 1964. *Fear of Flying*. New York: NAL.

Kanin, Michael, and Ring Lardner. 1942. *Woman of the Year*. 20th Century Fox Films. Filmstrip.

Kerr, Barbara A. 1997. *Smart Girls*, rev. ed. *A New Psychology of Girls, Women, and Giftedness*. Scottsdale, Arizona: Gifted Psy chol ogy Press.

Landrum, Gene N. 1999. *Eight Keys to Greatness: How to Unlock Your Hidden Potential*. Amherst, New York: Prometheus Books.

Leon ard, Linda . 1998. *The Wounded Woman: Healing the Father- Daughter Relationship*. Boston: Shambhala Publications.

Lowe, Jane. 1998. *Oprah Winfrey Speaks: Insight from the World's Most Influential Voice*. New York: John Wiley and Sons.

Martin, Katherine. 1999. *Women of Courage: Inspiring Stories from the Women Who Lived Them.* Novato, California: New World Library.

Morrison, Toni. 1987. *Beloved.* New York: Alfred A. Knopf.

Norman, Elizabeth M. 1999. *We Band of Angels: The Untold Story of American Nurses Trapped on Bataan by the Japanese.* New York: Random House.

Parks, Rosa (with Gregory J. Reed). 1994. *Quiet Strength: The Faith, The Hope, and the Heart of a Woman Who Changed a Nation.* Grand Rapids, Michigan: Zondervan Publishing House.

Person, Ethel S. 1989. *Dreams of Love and Fateful Encounters: The Power of Romantic Passion.* New York: Penguin.

Pipher, Mary. 1994. *Reviving Ophelia: Saving the Selves of Adolescent Girls.* New York: Ballantine.

Riso, Don Richard. 1990. *Understanding the Enneagram: The Practical Guide to Personality Types.* Boston: Houghton Mifflin.

Russell, Willy. 1989. *Shirley Valentine.* Paramount Pictures. Film.

Scott, Steven K. 1998. *Simple Steps to Impossible Dreams: The 15 Power Secrets of the World's Most Successful People.* New York: Simon and Schuster.

Tavris, Carol. 1989. *Anger: The Misunderstood Emotion.* New York: Simon and Schuster.

Valentis, Mary, and Anne Devane. 1994. *Female Rage: Unlocking Its Secrets, Claiming Its Power.* New York: Carol Southern Books/ Crown.

Viscott, David. 1977. *Risking.* New York: Pocket Books.

———. 1996. *Emotional Resilience: Simple Truths for Dealing with the Unfinished Business of Your Past.* New York: Crown Publishers.

Wachowski Bros. 1999. *The Matrix.* Warner Bros. Film.

Mary Valentis, Ph.D., teaches writing, literature, popular culture, and literary theory at the State University of New York at Albany. A former reporter and columnist for the Hearst Newspapers, she is the coauthor of *Female Rage: Unlocking Its Secrets, Claiming Its Power,* and the editor of *The American Sublime.* Dr. Valentis has published numerous articles in such magazines as *New Woman* and in scholarly journals and collections. A worldwide consultant and lecturer, her classes, retreats, and workshops focus on women's issues, romantic love, trauma writing, and popular culture.

John Valentis, Ph.D., has been involved in the mental health field for over twenty-five years. A clinical hypnotist and psychotherapist who specializes in motivation, relationships, and the psychology of health, he is the host of the popular call-in advice program, *The Dr. John Valentis Show.* Dr. Valentis also presents training seminars on various mental health issues, and on skill enhancement for physicians and mental health practitioners.

Some Other
New Harbinger Titles

Pregnancy Stories, Item PS $14.95

The Women's Guide to Total Self-Esteem, Item WGTS $13.95

Thinking Pregnant, Item TKPG $13.95

The Conscious Bride, Item CB $12.95

Juicy Tomatoes, Item JTOM $13.95

Facing 30, Item F30 $12.95

The Money Mystique, Item MYST $13.95

High on Stress, Item HOS $13.95

Perimenopause, 2nd edition, Item PER2 $16.95

The Infertility Survival Guide, Item ISG $16.95

After the Breakup, ATB $13.95

Claiming Your Creative Self, Item CYCS $15.95

The Self-Nourishment Companion, Item SNC $10.95

Serenity to Go, Item STG $12.95

Spiritual Housecleaning, Item SH $12.95

Goodbye Good Girl, Item GGG $12.95

Under Her Wing, Item WING $13.95

Goodbye Mother, Hello Woman, Item GOOD $14.95

Consuming Passions, Item PASS $11.95

Binge No More, Item BNM $14.95

The Mother's Survival Guide to Recovery, Item MOM $12.95

Women's Sexualities, Item WOSE $15.95

Undefended Love, Item UNLO $13.95

Call **toll free, 1-800-748-6273,** or log on to our online bookstore at **www.newharbinger.com** to order. Have your Visa or Mastercard number ready. Or send a check for the titles you want to New Harbinger Publications, Inc., 5674 Shattuck Ave., Oakland, CA 94609. Include $4.50 for the first book and 75¢ for each additional book, to cover shipping and handling. (California residents please include appropriate sales tax.) Allow two to five weeks for delivery.

Prices subject to change without notice.